4608 A

Harold Martin Remembers

CATS DOGS CHILDREN
and other SMALL CREATURES

Illustrated by INEZ ROSKOS

 Peachtree Publishers, Ltd.

Published by
PEACHTREE PUBLISHERS, LTD.
494 Armour Circle, N. E.
Atlanta, Georgia 30324

Copyright © 1980 Harold H. Martin, Text
                  Inez Roskos, Illustrations

All rights reserved. No part of this book may be reproduced in any form or by any means without the prior written permission of the Publisher, excepting brief quotes used in connection with reviews, written specifically for inclusion in a magazine or newspaper.

Manufactured in the United States of America.

Library of Congress Cataloging in Publication Data

Martin, Harold H
  Cats and dogs, children, and other small creatures.

  1. Pets—Legends and stories. 2. Animals, Legends and stories of. 3. Martin, Harold H. I. Title.
SF416.M37   818'.5403   80-23035
ISBN 0-931948-12-6

To all the readers who for forty years have shared with me stories of their own house cats, yard dogs, birds, squirrels, chipmunks, and children, these essays are affectionately dedicated.

H.M

Acknowledgements

I am deeply indebted to Dr. William Schaffer and his lady, Lee, who bore the burden of picking out from tattered scrapbooks those reminiscences that they felt would be of interest; and to Jim Rankin upon whom fell the burden of making the final choice. And finally, to all those who heard about this project, and dug deep into old dresser drawers and came up with yellowed clippings of columns that had pleased them, or their mothers, which they hoped they might see in print again.

H.M.

Contents

And Now the House Is Empty	1
The Back-Fence Troubadour	3
"... And Make a Dignified Exit"	6
Cold Thermometer Heats Up Tomcat	10
Dogs and Men Chasing Butterflies	13
His Head Was Stuck in the Wheaties Box	16
Old Shim Fights His Best Friend	19
With Pansy, Midnight Is on His Own	21
Fronto Learns the Hard Way	24
Little Guys Can Get Awfully Jealous	27
The Cat in the Snow	30
New Members of the Household	33
Midnight Misses a Role in *Alice*	37
The Case of the Bridge-Player's Cat	40
Cured for the Time, Anyway	43
When Blue Jay Fails to Notice Cat, Spring Is Here	46
Everybody Was Glad Except the Cat	48
Only Captain Midnight Missing Upon Return From Far Pacific	51
To Get Rid of Spiders, Shake Their Ears Off	54
The Wily Ways of Our Progeny	56
A Rooster Trio Crows at Dawn	59
"Bub" Not So Bad, After All	61

Let the Doctor Explain the Mysteries of Manhood	64
He Can't Keep From Brawling	67
Mr. McGill Joins the Fancy	70
Wherever He Is, Smokey Deserves the Best	73
Mockingbirds Have a No-Cat Zone	76
How to Drive a Parent Crazy	78
Peace Can Be Lonely, Too	81
"Claire de Lune" Put Brewster to Sleep	84
The First Warm Winds of Spring	86
Shim Misses His Snoozing Place	88
Anybody Need a Squirrel?	90
Shim Comes Back Into the Family	93
Brewster Finds His Harem in the Hills	95
Chester and the Cat Show	97
He Never Lost a Fight	100
Swaggering Mouse Stole the Kleenex	102
Chester Had to Have His Rest	104
That Sad and Happy Last Day	107
Broadus the Cat Buffaloes Dogs	110
The Green Dean Comes to Live	112
School Days Start the Morning Storms	114
Old Galahad Adjusts to His New Home	117
He Was Always Losing Something	119
A Parrot Wants His Coffee	121
Courting in the Mountain Rain	123
Parrots Talk a Lot, But Say Little	126

It Was a Long Journey, in More Ways Than One	128
Galahad Spoke Too Soon	131
Graduation Was a Time for Pride	135
Things Said at Times When You Don't Know What to Say	137
Pet Raccoon Trees Mr. Cox	139
A Man Wants His Freedom at Twenty-One	143
Weddings Disrupt Lives of Fathers and Small Dogs	145
Sourpuss Better Mind His Manners	148
Sourpuss Soared Into a Rosebush	150
He Needed Help to Pass the Cat	152
The Old and the Gray	154
Small Speckled Bird Found Dazed on Sidewalk	159
Old Shim Knew His Time Had Come	161
The Queen's First Birthday	164
Idiot Towhee Feeds Cowbirds As if They Were Her Own	167
The King Is Gone; Long Live the King	169
Fat Tassie Forgives	171
Queen's new Trick Guaranteed to Make Anybody Feel Silly	174
The Years Fall Away	176
Just Sit Back and Enjoy	179

Foreword

Ralph McGill invited Harold Martin and me to meet his old friend, Carl Sandburg, when the poet once paid him a visit in Atlanta. The four of us had lunch in a private room at the Capital City Club where we then spent the afternoon telling stories and listening to Sandburg play his guitar and sing his songs (we declined the old minstrel's offer to share some of the brandy and goat's milk he'd brought in his satchel). At the end of the day, Sandburg shook Martin's hand and peered at him intently for a moment.

"There is music in what you write," Carl Sandburg said simply to Harold Martin.

The melody and the cadence of the English language did reveal themselves uncommonly to the big bear of a Georgian who looks like a linebacker and thinks like a saint (except when the devils of bawdy irreverence take him, and they dwell near his surface).

Nature joined a strong arm to a gentle spirit in him and coupled there a sensitive reverence for life with an antic gift of fun.

He roamed the world for many years from his Atlanta base to write his brilliant articles for the old *Saturday Evening Post*. No magazine writer in mid-century America excelled him. He wrote of men and nations and momentous happenings with the expert authority springing from that rarest virtue among writers, an apolitical and open mind, which brings no burden of pretense or partisanship to events. He looked upon his times with the fresh wonder of the unconvinced. Popular passions never swayed his inquiries. They simply puzzled him. He was only looking for the truth. So he thought originally, and judged wisely, and wrote in perfect pitch.

Yet another Harold Martin lived in the editorial pages of The *Atlanta Constitution*. Unlike the cosmic issues he wrote about for the *Post*, the pieces he wrote for The *Constitution* were the little stories of his home and private life, detached from his larger searches.

Thus it was that The *Constitution's* readers came to know a subject larger than his separate works, the real Harold Martin. And the little essays from his private life may prove to live long after his stories of wars and presidents are, like the national magazine which published them, dead.

This book's sampling discloses the man through his friendship with children and chipmunks and old dog Shim, with squirrels and birds and many cats (Chester, Old Sourpuss, Sir Galahad, and Captain Midnight, "the Adolph Menjou of the back fence troubadours"). Then there was his rooster, Brewster. Even the dogs of neighbors adopted Martin, who took formal care to accord them always their families' names (Fat Tassie Fitzsimmons).

So read this relaxed book as it was written, happily. But do not be deceived by Martin's claim that it is just about "cats and dogs and children and all manner of creatures, great and small."

The small stories he tells here reveal the great spirit of a human being of particular value. And there is music in what he writes.

Eugene Patterson
St. Petersburg, Florida
August 4, 1980

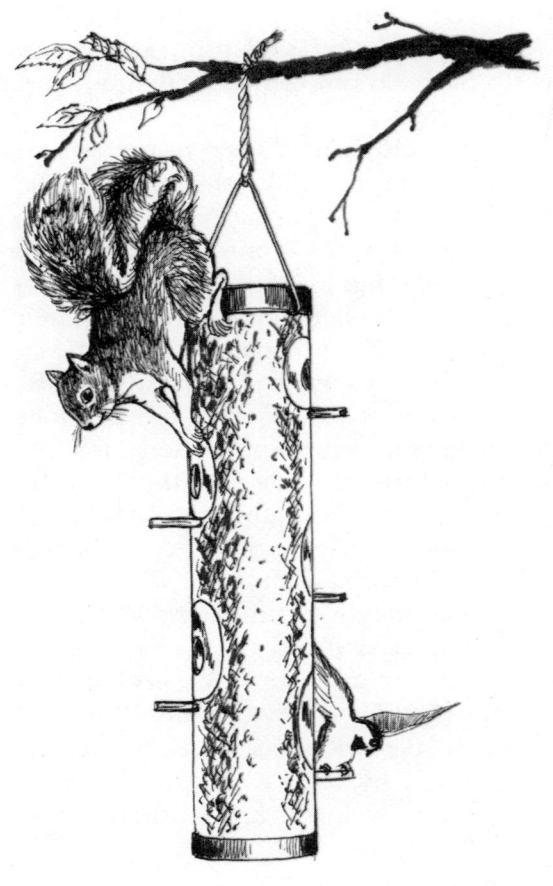

And Now the House Is Empty . . .

The last one is gone now.

With her nose a little red from a cold, and her eyelids a little red from crying, we loaded her and her clothes and all her treasures into the car and packed her off on a rainy Sunday morning to college and a new life.

Now the house is empty of children for the first time in nearly twenty-five years, and Mama and I are back where we were before the first baby came—just the two of us.

It's going to take a little getting used to—this unfamiliar stillness.

No water running in the shower upstairs, no voices murmuring and giggling on the telephone, no thunder of footsteps on the stair, no beat and throb of folk music coming from behind the closed doors where they're supposed to be studying. No shouting, no quarreling—and no laughter.

Just lonely silence, broken by the little sounds we never noticed before, the small squeaks and thumpings that an empty house makes when it cools at the end of the day.

So another milestone passes on that long road a man begins to travel when he stands up, moist of palm, and knees atremble, and the preacher asks the question, and he answers in a frog-like croak, "I do."

We'd looked forward to it all these years, this time that is both sad and happy, when they all had gone. But just as each baby brings its love with it when it comes, each, when the time comes to go, leaves a great emptiness behind.

But you can't hold onto them, and you wouldn't if you could. For to them this leaving is a milestone, too, in the long road they walk.

And the one thing that every parent learns is that every generation walks its own road alone.

I think that Miss Eva, who came to us when the one who was leaving was just a baby, said best what I'm trying to say. In a little note she scrawled and hid beneath a pillow she wrote:

"For Nancy: Well, Miss Twink, it has been much fun down through the years watching you grow up into a Beautiful and very nice young lady. We have had a lovely time together, now the time has come when the Best of Friends will have to part, as much as they hate to. But the large and lovely world has a place for every one of its people, and it is up to him or her to go out and find a place in the world. I guess you know today has been a very hard one for me. I just can't keep back the tears from showing. I will miss you so much, so please do a good job and find your place as all the others. I know you will, Twink. I think Parents are like birds. They love their little ones and take care of them, but soon they have to let them go. My Carl says every boy and girl has to find his place in the world himself. Can't nobody do this for him. That's pretty good thinking on his part. Please excuse me, you understand me. I love and will miss you very much. Love Eva."

In this "large and lovely world" each child does have to find his place. And I'm learning that parents have to find a new place, too, once they are gone.

The Back-Fence Troubadour

Years ago I owned a fine black tomcat named Captain Midnight who was held in high esteem by all who knew him. He was as gay a caballero, I guess, as ever the feline tribe produced, ever ready to sing a song or go aroaming in the gloaming, or fight for a lady's hand, whichever seemed the thing to do at the moment.

Every night about moonrise he would come to me, green eyes gleaming, and meow to be let out. So I'd open the back door and, with ever the faintest pause to sniff the wind for a possible lurking dog, he would set out on his social ramble.

Moving with the jauntiness of a boulevardier in top hat and tails, he would set out across the moonlit lawn, a drift of black and silver smoke, until all at once he was not there. And every morning he would come meowing to be let in, still dapper, still debonair, still jauntily twirling his moustache and swinging an imaginary cane, the Adolph Menjou of the back-fence troubadours.

All of the other cats I ever put out at my back door at night, even the incomparable Chester, Jr., always came back muddy, bloody, scarred, and limping. Old Midnight did that only once; usually he came back with a swagger, every hair in place. It may be that he was not a fighting cat, but I don't think this is the case. I think he put down lesser cats by sheer hauteur. He didn't have to fight the toms or woo the ladies. He prevailed just by being there. How serenely he passed his evenings out is evidenced by the fact that on one morning he came home wearing my watch.

What happened was, I'd been reading in my chair and old Midnight had come by and rubbed against my leg, and without thinking I'd slipped my wristwatch with the expandable band over his head. Then I'd forgotten it until bedtime. By that time it was too late. One of the kids, not noticing, had let Midnight out the back door with my watch around his neck. It is the only time I ever got up at daylight to greet a homecoming tomcat.

All this nostalgic outpouring about my old cat Captain Midnight was brought on by a letter from a very nice lady named Mary Ellen Murray, who writes from Gainesville, Georgia, that some years ago while she was at Emory, she did her masters thesis on Ralph McGill's editorials. This meant that she had to read The *Atlanta Constitution's* editorial page every day, and the op-ed page on which these essays appeared.

"I formed the habit of reading your column," she said, "and I developed a great affection for your cat, Captain Midnight. Since then, I married an army officer and have spent ten years wandering over the world. Now, I am back, living in Gainesville, and to find Ralph McGill no longer on the front page, and your home bereft of pets, is a solemn experience. So please, tell me about Captain Midnight, and how he fared, and where he is."

To which I can only answer that one night he went out as usual and never came back again, and what happened to him I've never known. But I'm pretty sure that somewhere out there on some high celestial back fence that separates the backyards of the stars, he is striding back and forth, still singing his love songs to the moon, and twirling his whiskers, and swinging his cane with the oldtime jauntiness of a boulevardier in top hat and tails, forever.

"... And Make a Dignified Exit"

Mama and I had a little fuss the other morning, and as a result I am limping heavily on one leg today, and it is no pleasure to sit down unless there is a very soft cushion in the seat. That, I know, sounds very much as if she gave me a good going over with a baseball bat. It was not quite as bad as that, and maybe I had better explain.

What happened was the same thing which happens around nearly everybody's house, I guess. It was the old, old battle about how you should go about disciplining the younguns, so that they will do what you tell them without getting mad or sulky about it, and how you can handle small rebels without losing your temper and with it your dignity.

One of the boys had doped off as usual. He had come in to breakfast without combing his hair and washing his face and hands, and she had spoken to him about it, as she has had to do, I suppose, every morning since he got big enough to dress himself. So she already was a little sore. Then she went upstairs for a moment, and there was his room, looking as if a cyclone had just blown through it, with all the dresser drawers open and atumble, and a pair of tennis shoes in the middle of the floor, and a basketball on the dresser, and—well, you know how a small boy's room is.

Then, when she came back downstairs, he was at the table again, eating his crispies, or sparkies, or zoomies, or whatever silly name they call that particular kind of breakfast food, and his hands were washed pretty well, though they still looked a little like the paws of a black cub bear, as all small boys' hands look in the wintertime, for they don't ever dry their hands well, and they get chapped, and dirt gets ground into the chapped knuckles. They weren't so bad, though. It was his face. It was obvious he had not touched his face with water because it was all smudged and gooey looking.

So she got pretty sore, and spoke to him with great sharpness along the lines of how many times she had to tell him about these things and when will he ever learn to be neat and like a human being instead of like a small pig.

So I stuck my nose into it, though I should have had more sense. And I said, "Now, now, Mama, let us not raise our voice in such a querulous manner. When you lose your temper you destroy the effect of what you are trying to say, for a small boy has the faculty of being able to shut his ears and his mind to what you are saying to him when you are angry. He just sits there until the storm blows over, snuffling and full of woe, but really not paying attention, because he has withdrawn within his shell, like a terrapin."

"Phooey to you and your terrapins," she says to me, her eyes snapping with anger. "It seems to me you would try to help me when I am correcting the children instead of taking their side every time . . . ."

"I am not taking their side," I insist. "I am just trying to point out how these things should be done. Speak in a low, quiet, firm voice, and say what you have to say and then walk away with dignity. Do not ever let your dignity suffer. It is of great importance that you always maintain a calm, sedate bearing when correcting the children."

"All right," she said. "I am going to let you handle the discipline for a while. I want to see a demonstration of this dignified rebuke you are always talking about."

The situation is still strained when I come home from the office, and I am very happy to learn that some friends are going to come by after supper, for you have to be nice to each other when outsiders are present; and often, when you are nice to each other for a whole evening, you forget what you were mad about.

So it works out this way, and we sit around chatting very pleasantly, until all of a sudden upstairs a horrible fuss breaks out. There is the sound of thumps and stampings, and voices raised high in anger, and the slamming of doors.

I sit there, waiting for her to go up to quell the disturbance, but she does not move. She just smiles at me with poisonous sweetness, and nods toward the stair, and I know that I am under the gun and will have to take the situation in hand.

So I rise and excuse myself to my guests and march up the stairs in a dignified manner, into the middle of the bedlam.

"Here, here," I say, in a low, well-modulated, but firm voice. "What goes on here?"

So they all start trying to talk at once, but I raise my hand peremptorily.

"One at the time," I say, quietly but firmly.

Well, it seems that the fight starts because my oldest daughter keeps a diary, and the boys have sneaked into her room and swiped the diary, and have been going about reading passages from it aloud, and she has tried to retrieve the book by force, and in the scuffle it has been torn, and she is angry at this, and has pasted them both a good one on the snoot.

So I consider the evidence in the case and hand down my decision. The boys are forbidden to enter her room again, and they must pay for the torn-up diary.

CATS AND DOGS, CHILDREN AND OTHER SMALL CREATURES

"Yes, sir," they said.

"Now all of you go to your rooms," I said.

"Yes, sir," they said.

So, feeling very proud of myself for the quiet, forceful, yet dignified manner in which I have handled the situation, I turn to descend the stair. I still don't know what happened. All I know is that my feet fly out from under me and I start down, flat of my back, sliding as if I am on a sled, with every stair tread raking along my spine. I clutch frantically at the smooth walls, but to no avail, and the first thing I know I hit the bottom and scoot across the entrance hall, which is floored with highly waxed linoleum, still going with great velocity, until I fetch up against the wall on the other side.

And I remember noting the look of startled amazement on the faces of my spouse and my guests as I whiz past the entrance to the living room, and their shrill cry of alarm which is soon replaced by bellows of laughter which shake the house.

And as I rise and stagger weakly to peer up the stair, trying to see what it was that caused my sudden swift descent, there is my whole brood, hanging over the rail, laughing as if in all their lives they had never seen anything as funny as their papa falling downstairs.

But the worst of it is that as I limp back to the living room and sink painfully into a chair, my wife is still laughing so hard there are tears in her eyes as big as lemons.

"Say what you have to say, quietly and firmly," she gasped, quoting me. "And then make a dignified exit."

Cold Thermometer Heats Up Tomcat

Mr. Agnew Coker, who works for the city of Atlanta at the Sandy Creek sewage disposal plant, called up the other morning to ask me if I ever heard what Voltaire said about cats. I hadn't, so he told me. He said Voltaire said: "I wonder if my cat gets as much fun out of watching me as I get out of watching my cat."

He then went on to tell me what happened the time his wife took his tomcat, Figaro, to the veterinarian.

He said his wife told the veterinarian he had better watch out, because Figaro was the meanest tomcat that ever lived. He loved her, and he loved children, but he hated dogs and everybody else, and he would not only claw them, he would chew them up.

The veterinarian just laughed. He never saw a cat he couldn't handle, he said.

"Now," he said, "we will take his temperature."

"You better watch out," Mrs. Coker told the vet. "He'll bite your thermometer in two."

"Madam," the vet said, "that is not how we take a cat's temperature. Lay him down on that table."

So she laid Figaro down on the table and the vet took his

thermometer and shook it, and he started to take Figaro's temperature.

Mrs. Coker still does not know exactly what happened. She noticed that Figaro's tail was twitching angrily as the doctor poked the thermometer at him. Then things got kind of blurry and confused. Somehow, all of a sudden the doctor was up on the table, doing some sort of wild dance, and blood was showing through his white coat, and Figaro was on top of the doctor's head, digging his claws in, and the doctor was shouting and stomping on his spectacles, which had fallen off on the table.

Then Figaro took off from the doctor's skull in a flying leap, through an open door which led into the operating room, and there was a crash of glass and metal, and she rushed in, and Figaro had knocked over the cabinet where the doctor had kept his instruments. He had also knocked over the thing the instruments are sterilized in, and there was hot water all over the place, and she thinks Figaro must have got some of this hot water on his person, for he made another wild leap through another door, into the waiting room, and there was another crash as he knocked a lamp off a table and he leaped from the table to the mantelpiece and knocked a clock and a picture of a basket of puppies off the mantelpiece onto the floor. So she ran into the waiting room and there was Figaro up on the valance over the window.

Then a couple of attendants wearing big leather gauntlets ran in and started trying to grab Figaro. And she does not know yet how Figaro and the two helpers, and the venetian blind from the window, all got down on the floor together, but they did. And with him all tangled up in the venetian blind, they finally got a hold on Figaro with the heavy gloves, and they wrapped him up in a towel so tight he looked like a mummy.

The doctor, who was all scratched and bleeding, took Figaro back into the examination room holding him like he was carrying a loaded A-bomb, and took his temperature. He did not have any fever.

I told Mr. Coker I'll bet what Voltaire said about cats wasn't half as interesting as what the doctor said about Figaro.

"He didn't say anything," Mr. Coker said. "He just handed Figaro back to my wife, still wrapped up in a towel.

" 'Lady,' he said, 'don't you EVER bring this cat back here again.' "

Dogs and Men Chasing Butterflies

It appears that I am going to have to revise my estimate of which of my dog friends is the most foolish dog in the world. For a considerable time the title undoubtedly belonged to a big red Irish setter named Shamus O. Bryan. Shamus, who lives up in the mountains, was the dog that let the deer make a monkey out of him by running away from him in relays until he was panting like a lizard, with his tongue dragging the ground and his feet all sore. But Shamus pretty soon got too smart for this sort of thing. He now waits until some of the mountain dogs jump a deer and then he lies happily on the front porch, listening to the sounds of the chase, until he is sure which way the deer is heading. Then he moves out in a leisurely manner to intercept the deer and give it a great run. He never catches one, but he sometimes gets in very close, and he gives up when he is still fairly fresh, and goes back to lie down on the porch.

With Shamus showing these signs of intelligence, my new candidate for the world's most foolish canine then became my old friend Fronto Creighton-Toombs, a big knuckleheaded English bulldog who lives down the street from me and who formerly spent a great deal of his time chasing my cat. I did not criticize Fronto Creighton-Toombs for chasing my cat, for that is a natural thing, and there was always a chance that he would catch the cat, though personally I think he would regret it sorely if he ever did.

Anyway, Fronto has given up chasing the cat, in which pursuit he had some small chance of success, and has now taken up chasing squirrels, in which he has no chance whatsoever. I have observed Fronto and the squirrels in action for the past two weeks, and it is my considered opinion that the squirrels are making him look silly. They come down to about three feet off the ground, standing upside down on the tree, and there they chatter and chatter until Fronto comes plowing through the underbrush in pursuit. Then they dart back up the tree, just high enough to be out of his reach when he jumps at them, and there they sit and insult him horribly, while he goes into a frenzy, leaping and barking and blunting his claws scratching at the tree. Sometimes they leap through the air above his head while he is leaping up at them and this causes him to try to turn in midair, and he gets all tangled up with himself and comes down with a crash, to the great amusement, no doubt, of the squirrels.

The silliest thing he does, though, is to try to chase them while they are leaping from limb to limb in the air. They go swinging along like small gray Tarzans, chattering happily, and below them Fronto goes kiyoodling through the underbrush, looking up instead of paying attention to where he is going and thus banging his head against small trees and skinning himself up considerably.

Which undoubtedly would make any thinking man consider Fronto Creighton-Toombs a little daft.

But now comes Shamus O. Bryan, who outdoes himself to become even stupider than Fronto. Shamus has taken up the sport of chasing the shadows of butterflies. Not the butterflies themselves, mind you, but their shadows, flitting over the grass. He will be lying there half asleep and a butterfly will pass over and cast its shadow in his vicinity and he will rise from his torpor and make a great leap at the shadow, which of course is not there, a butterfly changing course as the whim strikes it. He has been known to go leaping and pouncing all over the yard, trying to pin down the shadow of a butterfly, and on one occasion he followed this shadow right down to the swamp beside the stream, plunging off a grassy bank with a great splash, right into the muck.

Sometimes, of course, when the butterfly swoops low enough, Shamus notices it, and starts pursuing the butterfly itself, leaping straight up in the air and coming down, kerwhump, on his back, and in all sorts of awkward positions, until he is bruised, sore, and bewildered. Which makes him the uncontested champion among dogs who are a little soft in the head.

Somehow, though, the thought strikes me that I cannot too greatly low-rate my canine friends for their zeal in pursuing will-o-the-wisps which elude them. We are all in the same boat. Out my window I can see the tall buildings, the banks, and business houses of downtown. And they are full of people who are frenziedly pursuing the shadows of butterflies and the ghostly shapes of deer that run forever beyond their reach. Though they think of these things in terms of money and prestige and success.

Sometimes, unlike our canine friends, we catch a few of the things we chase so earnestly—a raise in pay, a better job, a new car, a new house, a fur coat for Mama—if we run hard enough, and leap high enough, and have a little luck. But at the end of the chase we are pretty bruised and sore and exhausted and bewildered, too. And immediately we begin chasing butterflies again.

His Head Was Stuck in the Wheaties Box

People who do not care about rabbits might as well turn on to another page, for I am full of information about rabbits. In fact, after about a week of being housebound, I do not know anything about anything else but rabbits, and cats, and children—except what I read in the papers, which is mainly about Henry Wallace, and, though I am aware that Mr. Wallace is more important than a whole pen full of rabbits, he is not as entertaining.

What I was going to talk about was the other morning when the rabbit got his head stuck in the Wheaties box, and the effect this misadventure had on my cat, Captain Midnight. Ever since the rabbit came to my house, some time during the Easter season, the cat has been very jealous of the rabbit. When the children pick the rabbit up and cuddle him and coo to him and talk baby talk to him, the cat, who up to now has been the recipient of these affections, gets in a jealous rage and stalks about the room, uttering loud, shrill meows, and pretty soon he goes over to the door and meows to be let out as if he can't stand the sight of such taking-on over a rabbit.

So the cat, in his rage, has been glaring malevolently at

the rabbit. He sits over in the corner putting the evil eye on the rabbit, who ignores him, and every time the rabbit hops about the house, chewing up the broom and nibbling shoestrings and curtains and slipcovers and the other strange edibles he seems to be so fond of, the cat stalks along behind him, with his eyes hot with anger and his tail twitching in rage. He looks all tense as if he is ready to spring at any moment, but so far he never has.

Anyway, the other morning, the usual morning trip to the grocery store is made, and the rabbit, being a member of the family, goes along and on the way home he is sitting in the back seat, and on the seat beside him is one of these breakfast food assortments—about six little boxes full of different kinds of dried hay and whatnot that are supposed to make children strong like radio cowboys. And from the front seat they hear a rustling of paper bags and look back and the rabbit is sitting up on his hind legs in the back seat and is busily gnawing the top off of a box of Wheaties. Naturally, since he has gone to so much trouble to get the top off the Wheaties, the cook feels that he should have them, so at home she puts the box of Wheaties down on the floor in the pantry closet so the rabbit can eat them. And the rabbit eats his way down into the box of Wheaties until his head is stuck down in the box so deep only the tips of his ears are sticking out.

About this time the cat, which does not care to go to the grocery store, comes stalking into the kitchen looking for the rabbit so he can follow him about, glaring and switching his tail. And just about the time the cat enters the kitchen the rabbit discovers that his head is stuck in the Wheaties box, and he comes bounding out of the pantry closet in a frenzy, with the box on his head, straight at the cat. Naturally, the cat is wildly alarmed at this apparition and leaps completely over the washing machine in his effort to escape, tearing out of the room with his tail all buzzed up and his claws digging into the linoleum.

HAROLD MARTIN REMEMBERS

As the cat disappears, the rabbit finally controls himself long enough to sit up on his hind legs and bat the Wheaties box off his head with his front paws. Then he sits there, wiggling his nose and looking foolish.

And now the cat does not stalk along behind the rabbit any more, looking as if he would like to tear him up. In fact, he will not even stay in the same room with the rabbit.

Old Shim Fights His Best Friend

Some scientists up at the University of Michigan have spent a lot of time and money finding out something most folks knew all along—that animals have a deep sense of property rights and that they pursue a strict "paws off" policy where their own possessions are concerned. Some animals, like squirrels, they point out, protect the trees where they've stored their food supplies.

Others, like muskrats and beavers, don't worry so much about food, but they fight anything that comes around the place where they live. Even little fellows like mice and chipmunks will stand up and fight a trespasser; and seals, the professors say, lay claim to certain ice floes which they will defend as their own.

The most resolute guardsman of his own territory, the professor points out, is man's old friend, the dog.

This, of course, is so, and a man who owns a dog must recognize this fact when he expects to add to his collection of pets. When old Galahad, my tomcat, came to my house to live, my dog Shim's first impulse was to eat him up.

We had to have long talks with Shim, explaining to him

about Galahad and threatening him with bodily harm if he did not leave Galahad alone.

So now he ignores Galahad, paying him no more attention than if he were an ant, a falling leaf, a bird passing by in flight. But the cat has become part of the household and, as such, he must be defended.

The other afternoon, for example, I put this theory to the test.

We are sitting on the terrace, the dog, the cat, and I, when I see old Smokey, the dog from down the street, stride up the driveway. I pick up the cat and slip into the house with him and just as Smokey passes by the kitchen door to christen the shrubbery there, as is his custom, I drop the cat on his back. There is a great yowling and howling and snarling and leaping and the cat streaks across the terrace with Smokey in hot pursuit.

And they pass right by old Shim, who rises in his rage and leaps upon old Smokey, the best friend he's got in the world, and mauls him most severely for chasing his bitterest enemy, the cat.

With Pansy, Midnight Is on His Own

Down in the woods back of my house, a place sweet with birdsong in the morning, where small and amiable creatures, such as squirrels and chipmunks, frisk about, a murderous feud is being waged that sometime soon is going to end in death.

The protagonists in this silent, shadowy war are my cat, Captain Midnight, young and vigorous, but not yet aroused to a killing pitch, and an old battle-scarred tomcat with the strangely inappropriate name of Pansy.

Pansy belongs to a friend and neighbor, and I remember him as a kitten. The name then fitted, for he was the softest, prettiest little flower-faced fellow you ever saw, dark around the muzzle and the eyes, tawny about the throat and ears.

I don't know what happened to him to make him go bad. He was raised in the lap of luxury. He had the run of a beautiful house, all the milk he could drink, kind words from all who knew him, and fish not only on Friday but during the week.

Somehow, though, he became embittered. Maybe it was because there were so many cats around. Every week or so one of his sisters or one of his aunts or even his mama would come up proudly with another litter of kittens, and it seemed to sour his disposition.

The male kittens in these new families started mysteriously disappearing. They would be seen wandering off happily down into the woods, tails aplume, to investigate beetles, field mice, and other small creatures, and then they would be seen no more. Finally my friends figured out that Pansy was the murderer. Their attitude toward Pansy changed. They grew suspicious of him. He seemed to sense their displeasure. He became less and less a house cat, and more and more a ranger of the woods.

He seemed to get no pleasure out of life except by fighting. Down in the woods at night you would hear his battle cry as he tangled with a husky nephew or cousin or brother. In one of these night battles he lost an eye. He became stiff and lame with scars. But he always won, and every victory seemed to make him more thirsty for battle.

Finally he started staying away from the house altogether. He lured a young lady cat away from the quiet fireside to share his lone and angry life, and they live together now somewhere deep in the woods. Sometimes, as if lonely for the old life, she comes back and mews to be let in the kitchen. But she seems unhappy there, walking about and crying loudly. When she cries this way Pansy comes stalking up out of the woods, his good eye gleaming. He stalks into the kitchen, goes over to her, mews and purrs and talks to her and she calms down immediately. Then he takes her back to the woods again.

Pansy ruled the neighborhood for a long time. Then Captain Midnight came along. He was a cat with gentle raising. Kids held him in their laps and made much of him. For a while he squalled and scratched when I wanted to put him out of the house. When he would hit the ground outside the door he would look all about him, as if he were reconnoitering, before he would venture away from the door. Sometimes he would head straight for the big oak tree at the corner of the yard and go up it, where he would sit looking at every bush and clump of grass below.

Lately he has been stalking out, looking neither to the right nor the left, and I have been hearing his war cry at night. He is, I think, losing a little of his fear of Pansy. He is beginning to tangle with Pansy once in a while. But the old cat has weight, and age, and fighting experience on his side. Midnight is not ready to make it a battle to the death yet. I saw him come up out of the woods the other afternoon like a black streak. The big tawny cat was hot on his tail. But Midnight turned in the yard and put his back up and spat like a wet firecracker. His claws were out like hooks. Pansy backed down and slunk away.

Sometime Midnight is going to figure the time has come to stand and fight. Then the night is going to be hideous with their cries, and one of them is not going to walk out of the woods. I hope it isn't Midnight. But I can't help him. I'll keep the kids from pulling his tail, but down there in the dark with Pansy, he's on his own.

Fronto Learns the Hard Way

Every afternoon about five o'clock, Mr. William Creighton's bulldog, Fronto, comes up to my house to chase my cat up a tree. It has been going on for about two months now, and I think they both get a great deal of pleasure out of it. The cat comes and sits there on the back step, licking her coat and looking about and yawning and stretching, but all the time keeping a sharp eye out, though pretending not to.

Fronto, a big brindle fellow, magnificently muscled about the shoulders, with a fine, clean-cut head on him, comes trotting up through Mr. Ben Shute's backyard until he gets to the edge of my estate, where he pauses and reconnoiters the terrain thoroughly. Then he begins to come on more slowly, stiff-legged and tense, until he gets to the corner of the house. He waits a minute, sniffing, and she, who maybe has heard the soft pad of his footsteps, tenses and sits perfectly still. Then, very slowly, he pokes his nose around the side of the house and looks her in the eye and she looks him in the eye, and her tail buzzes up; and he lunges, and she takes off like a black-and-white streak, with him right after her; and she hits the tree about three feet from the ground, with his nose almost touching the tip of her tail;

and he swerves just in time to keep from busting his brains out against the tree, and she pauses about ten feet up and looks down at him with a smug look on her face, greatly pleased with herself. He does not sit there, keeping her up the tree, but trots off home very nonchalantly, and she comes down and takes her place on the back step again, and pretty soon he comes creeping back and the whole process is repeated. They do this about three times until it gets dark and the cat comes in the house to get her supper, in fine fettle from the exercise, and Fronto goes home.

So far, she has never laid a paw on him, and he has never nipped so much as the tip of her tail, and the whole thing has been in a spirit, it seems to me, of good clean fun. But yesterday the whole pattern changed. The cat was sitting there waiting, and Fronto was creeping up, trembling in his eagerness, when one of the black kittens came out from under the automobile, pursuing a bug. The bug, a large, black bug, was getting over the ground with some speed, and the kitten, with its black tail sticking straight up in the air like a spike, was following right behind it, trying to make up its mind whether to make a pass at it or not. And the bug and the kitten got to the corner of the house just at the moment when Fronto stuck his nose around to see if the big cat was present and chasable.

Being a tall dog, and intent on his work, he didn't see the black kitten at first until he heard a vicious "fffft" coming from between his forepaws and he looked down suddenly and there was the kitten staring him right in the eye, with its back up and its tail abuzz, and before he could make a move, five tiny claws, sharp as fishhooks, took him right in the nose. It was the funniest thing you ever saw. He is still sort of puppyish and awkward and he couldn't get his feet coordinated, and he went straight up in the air and came down all asprawl with his legs churning and his big paws throwing gravel and dirt all over the place. And when he tried to make the turn around the other end of the house, headed for home, he hit a muddy place and skidded and shot, tail over tip, into a tangle of shrubbery and out of it on the other side all wet and muddy and plastered with leaves.

The kitten didn't seem to realize she had done anything at all remarkable, and went on pursuing the black bug very calmly, as if nothing had happened.

But the big cat took note of the phenomenon, and about an hour later, when Fronto finally got up enough courage to come back up there and find out what the dickens had happened the first time, the big cat was waiting for him. She pretended to be investigating something in the flower beds and she let him get so close she could have tickled his nose with her tail, when all of a sudden she whirled and went about four feet in the air, going "ZZZZTTTT ZZZZTTTT ZZZZTTTTT" like a short circuit in a high-voltage wire. Her claws must have looked as murderous as cotton hooks to Fronto, for by this time he was just a brindle streak through the woods, going home.

He didn't come back again yesterday, and I don't know whether he will be back or not. He is welcome to come if he wants to, but I will not be legally responsible for what happens. And I hope that his master, Mr. Creighton, will not look upon him as a poltroon for the way he handled himself. He was doing all right until the cats changed the rules on him.

Little Guys Can Get Awfully Jealous

What I should do is ponder over this question a long time and then write a profound psychological piece for *Parents* magazine or something. I refer to the current feud that is going on between me and my son, John, age four, who resents, in a way that I think he does not quite understand, my having come home to root him out of his long-held place as the man of the house.

It is a one-way feud, of course. He snipes at me, while I try to woo him into friendship, and it will soon blow over, I know. But I bet there are thousands of fathers back from the war who are having the same trouble in milder or more virulent form.

The trouble is, when I went away he was just a little fellow, just beginning to toddle around, not talking yet, and too young to know me as his father or to care whether I went away or not. In fact, Roy, the yardman, was closer to him than I was, because he toddled around after Roy all day, helping him polish doorknobs and rake leaves and seeing much more of Roy than he did of me, who was home to play with him only at night.

And while I was gone, since he was at the stage where he

enjoyed pulling things off tables, striking matches, breaking light switches with hammers and pouring glue in the seats of chairs, his mother, to save the house from complete destruction, would take him with her whenever she went out. Therefore he became her constant companion, at home and abroad. Whenever she got her coat to go, he got his. Then I came home. With me there to look after him, there was no need for him to go with his mama to the grocery store (a break for his mama, for little boys can get into even more trouble in grocery stores than they can get into at home).

Also, I started taking his mama out in the evenings, sometimes, which displeased him. And when I would come in from work in the evenings and would receive from my everloving spouse that brief perfunctory smacker with which wives greet their husbands, he would become very jealous. He would stand over in the corner and glower at me as if he would like to bite me on the leg. In fact, once he did bite me on the leg.

Finally, he got it off his chest. I was sitting in my chair one evening, thinking about nothing in particular, when he came over and looked me in the eye.

"I am going to frow you away," he said, "and get a new daddy."

I told him that I was very sad to hear that, and attempted to take him in my lap to find out the cause of his wrath at me. He did not wish to be so dandled. So I left him alone and went on just as I had been doing, treating him just like the rest of the youngsters, counting him in over their protests on all the games we played together (did you ever try to play Authors with a four-year-old boy who does not know Henry Wadsworth Longfellow from William Makepeace Thackeray?) and offering, or attempting to offer, only such extra affection as he would accept. He didn't accept much. He was fond of roughhousing on the floor, but I seemed to note a certain grim seriousness in his roughhousing that was lacking in the other children's sport. At least they never sneaked up on me from behind and rapped me on the skull with a short section of two-by-four which some manufacturer fondly thought resembled a train engine. And he did, twice.

Whether or not my campaign of kindliness has had anything to do with it or not, he has, of late, accepted me to the point where he will ask me to do things for him. He brings out an assortment of battered toys and asks me to tell him about the big airplane and about the little airplane and about the ship and the train, and I discourse on these subjects until I am blue in the face. And it seems as if all is well between us. Until I tell him that it is time for him to go to bed and he sticks out his lower lip and scowls at me and says, "No," and he refuses to budge. But when his mama says, "Bedtime, Johnny," he gathers up his gear and patters off without a squawk.

He is a smart little cookie, though. He knows that I am trying to get him to like me, so when he wants something that he is pretty sure his mama will not let him have, such as another piece of candy when he has had four pieces already, he always comes and asks me to get it for him.

Sometimes I almost forget that I am not yet quite accepted by him. Like the other night. We roughhoused very happily on the floor and he did not strike me with any blunt instruments, and I told him stories by the hour, and when finally I sent him off to get his bath he went without protest. He even came and kissed me goodnight along with the rest of the kids, a thing he had steadfastly refused to do before. And I thought, well, I guess I am in. I am Papa at last, instead of that big oaf that came in here and shoved him back to a subordinate spot in the household scheme. But I was wrong. Two hours later we were in a big battle. He had yelled for water, and I took him the water, and he wouldn't drink it. He said he wanted his mama to bring it to him and he wanted me to go away. The argument went on for quite some time. I guess he won it. Anyway, the water didn't end up in Johnny. It ended up in my shoe.

The Cat in the Snow

If Mrs. W. Blount Trammell thinks that her cat was surprised and pained when she slammed the refrigerator door on his tail by accident, she should have seen my cat, Captain Midnight, when I tossed him out the back door into the snow on purpose.

In order that the associated cat-lovers of Georgia do not fly into a rage, let me explain that I always toss the cat out the back door every morning. He likes it. He is too lazy to get up and follow me through the house and walk out the back door under his own steam. He likes to be carried back and tossed out.

Ordinarily, of course, he lights on the bare ground and goes about his business. The other morning he landed in the snow. He had never seen any snow, of course, being a Georgia cat, and you never saw such consternation on a cat's face in your life. He lit on his feet, naturally, and went up to his knees in the snow and he leaped stiff-legged straight up in the air about four feet, clawing at the air, and came down again and leaped again, this time toward the door, but I had already closed the door and was watching him through the glass. So he turned and went bounding across the yard, bouncing high in the air each time with his tail all buzzed up, until he got to the sliding board on the children's swing and he scooted up to the top of the slanting board and sat there taking stock of the situation. He had snow between his toes, which seemed to cause him great distress, and he would hold his foot up and look at it and shake it.

He was also reluctant to sit down, for it seems the snow was cold on his bottom, so he stood there a minute on the sliding board with his back all arched up, picking up first one foot and then the other. He looked like he was doing some sort of dance.

Then he began to calm down a little and notice what was going on. A few big flakes of snow were falling, drifting down lazily, and he was fascinated by these flakes. He would bat at them with his paw, trying to catch them, and they would land on his whiskers and his eyebrows and he would strike at them in a frenzy. Finally one came drifting down just out of reach and he batted at it, reaching far out, and he fell off the board into the snow, sending up a great flurry where he hit. He seemed to figure out then that it couldn't hurt him, and he began to play games in the snow.

He would run across the yard and put on brakes suddenly and skid, throwing up snow like a snowplow. There were a lot of little birds around, bouncing about on the snow, hunting weed seeds, and he started stalking these birds. Naturally, a coal-black cat moving across white snow might as well have a motorcycle escort with sirens announcing his coming, and he could not get close enough to the birds even to hurl an insult at them, much less catch one. One of them did booby-trap him, though. It lit in a rosebush and sat there watching him as he sneaked up, not moving a feather, and he leaped smack into the rosebush and got all tangled up in it, and he came out minus a few patches of fur. The bird, of course, was gone when he landed.

HAROLD MARTIN REMEMBERS

About that time a squirrel came out of the woods and sat there in the edge of the yard, looking at him, jerking its tail, and he took out after the squirrel. The squirrel turned and fled to a tree and scampered up and got to the first limb, which was covered with snow on top, and this caused the squirrel to lose his footing, so he fell out of the tree just as the cat got to the foot of it, and the squirrel lit right beside the cat. This so alarmed them both that they fled in opposite directions, the cat going up a small oak and the squirrel up a hickory beside it, and they sat there about six feet from each other, glaring in rage. Then the squirrel took off, leaping from branch to branch down through the woods, and the cat came home in disgust.

After that he went around to the front yard, where the kids had built a little snowman about a foot high, and he pranced up to the snowman, rearing up on his hind legs like a boxer, batting at the snowman. Then he grabbed at it like a wrestler and mauled it around, and the snowman went all to pieces, leaving the cat sitting there in a pile of snow, looking silly.

New Members of the Household

Through no volition of my own, I now find that two new members have attached themselves to my household. One is a terrapin of irascible disposition who thinks I am something to eat. The other is a frog. I do not know how long I am going to put up with this menagerié, but so far I have been able to get nowhere in my demands that this livestock be turned loose so that they can return to the deep tangled wildwood from whence they came and to which, no doubt, they would be willing to return.

The terrapin joined the family group, I admit, through my own mistaken sense of kindheartedness.

We are bowling down Habersham Road at a moderate rate of speed when I spy something that looks like a small, round-topped jewel box lying upside down in the middle of the road. Nobody else sees it, for the younguns, in the back of the car, are, as usual, either reading comic books or fighting about who is going to sit next to the window, and Mama is not watching the road, either, being busy trying to quell the riot going on about the window seats. I should have driven on, but, instead, I slow down and peer and see that the object in the road is a terrapin about the size of a soup plate. He is on his back and is waving his legs and putting out his head and threshing it about, trying to turn himself over.

Knowing that the next car which comes along will probably crush him into terrapin stew, I slam on the brakes, step out, turn him over and start to put him back by the side of the road, headed in the general direction of somebody's flower beds. At this, a great cry arises from the car, each child demanding that the terrapin be brought to him and that he be allowed to keep it as his own personal pet. I settle this by saying that we will keep the terrapin temporarily, the joint property of us all, until we can drop him off somewhere out in the country—Habersham Road, though a fine street populated by distinguished people, being obviously no proper home for a terrapin.

So we haul the terrapin off to the mountains with us and he makes a great nuisance of himself. He sulks in his shell until the children get tired of playing with him. Then they put him down on the floor of the car and the first thing I know he has crawled beneath my feet and is snapping at my ankle, trying to gnaw if off. I cannot much blame him for this, for everybody else in the car has had the forethought to put his feet up under him on the seat. Finally I get weary of trying to drive while defending myself against being maimed, and demand that they turn the terrapin over on his back in the car, so that he cannot wander about. Amazingly, though, he can flip himself over with ease in the car, merely by poking his neck out long and using it as a lever, a feat for some reason he did not seem able to accomplish on the street.

By the time we got to the mountain all chance of my getting rid of the terrapin, short of sneaking him off in the dead of the night and throwing him in the lake, was over. He had wormed his way into their affections by then, and they had resolved to keep him. As a result, I cannot sit in a chair, lie on a sofa, or even get into bed for a night of

CATS AND DOGS, CHILDREN AND OTHER SMALL CREATURES

well-earned repose without hearing a clump-clump-clump-clump along the floor and know that this beady-eyed monster is stalking me.

The frog, it seems, joined the household because of the terrapin. One of the smaller children, finding that the older ones had taken possession of the terrapin and were claiming it as their own, went out searching for something of his own to pet. He comes back with this large, clammy, bug-eyed toadfrog.

He does not mention that he has it, of course, and I am unaware such a beast is around the house until one morning I am at breakfast when I notice something wriggling in the shirt pocket of the small boy across the table. While I am staring wonderingly at this sight, something black catapults out of the pocket straight at me. I am about to take a sip of coffee at the moment and the sight of this projectile flying though the air startles me. I spill the coffee and the frog lands in it. The hot coffee naturally spurs him on to even longer leaps and he goes galumphing down the length of the table, turning over the sugar bowl, hopping into and out of a bowl of cereal, and in general causing a great uproar.

Naturally, I lay down the law at once, giving strict orders that both the frog and the terrapin must go. But at this a great howl goes up that I do not ever want them to have anything to play with and that their whole summer will be spoiled if I do not allow the beasts to remain and that they will not bring the frog to the table any more and that they will not forget and leave the turtle in the bedroom, and that, anyway, I have told them that they must always be kind to little helpless creatures.

So they have got me backed into a corner. But I am not licked yet. If I have any more trouble out of these monsters, I am going to take a drastic step. I am going to get Mr. Baker, down the mountain, to catch for me a large bullsnake, which I will insist upon my right to keep. Then

HAROLD MARTIN REMEMBERS

Mama, who so far has remained amazingly calm about the terrapin and the frog, will put her foot down and order all the animals off the place.

Midnight Misses a Role in *Alice*

My tomcat, Captain Midnight, has caused me bitter disappointment; but I cannot fuss at him too much about it, because I am partly at fault myself. I urged him to stand up and fight, and he did, and now he is absolutely worthless as an actor.

But the story is getting a little complicated so I had better start back at the beginning. The other day a very pleasant lady came into the office and started asking me questions about Captain Midnight. She wished to know what his color was, and I told her that he was black, as his name implies; and she inquired as to his disposition, and I told her that on the whole he had a splendid disposition, being of amiable and forgiving temperament, though now and then a little brusque with me.

She then inquired if he objected to being handled, and I told her that so far as I could tell he loved being handled more than any cat I ever saw. Half his life has been spent lolling in somebody's arms, purring happily, and if nobody seems disposed to fondle and pet him he will leap into their laps and rub his whiskers against their cheek, arching his back and insisting that they rub him.

As I gave this account of Captain Midnight's virtues, the lady's eyes grew bright and she broke into a wide smile.

"Mr. Martin," she said, "that is indeed wonderful news. I am Mrs. Norman W. Gibson, of the Atlanta Wesleyan Alumnae Club, and the ladies of the club have delegated me to investigate the character and background of Captain Midnight to see if he could be used as the cat which Alice carries about in her arms in the presentation of *Alice in Wonderland,* which the young ladies of Wesleyan are going to present at the Erlanger Theater on the evenings of March 20, 21, and 22.

"From what you say he is perfectly suited to the role of the cat in *Alice,* and we would all be so grateful if you would lend him to us to appear in the play. We will give him top billing, along with the stars of the play, and will notify the public that he is your cat, and both you and he will become famous around town."

So I go home and call happily for Captain Midnight, and he comes stalking up out of the woods and I was never so startled in my life. Great patches of fur are missing from his coat, one ear is torn and bloody, and he is matted with mud and briars and walks not with his usual jaunty insouciance, but with a truculent swagger, like Jack Dempsey. I reach down to pick him up and stroke him and he snarls at me and nips my hand and stalks off into the brush glowering back over his shoulder at me angrily.

While I am puzzling over this strange behavior and mourning this sad appearance of my once sleek and amiable cat, a neighbor from down the street calls for me to come down there. I go.

"Well," she said, "that piece you wrote about your cat having to stand up and fight my cat Pansy some time soon if he wished to keep his self-respect certainly bore fruit. Do you know what took place last night?"

"No," I said. "What?"

"Well," she said, "I was snoozing happily in my bed with

my cat Miss Priss, a very lovely lady cat, snoozing in her accustomed place at the foot of the bed, when I hear a meow and a 'bump,' and I look to see Pansy, my one-eyed and bad-tempered cat, sitting there observing Miss Priss and purring at her with affection. He had jumped in through the window. But before I have time to tell Pansy to go away and quit pressing his suit upon Miss Priss, there is another noise at the window, and who comes leaping through to land on my bed but your cat, Captain Midnight.

"Well, Pansy bows up in the back and goes 'Phhhht,' and Midnight bows up and goes 'Phhhhttt,' and then they explode into the d—dest cat fight you ever saw right on the foot of my bed, while Miss Priss, who cannot stand to witness such carnage, leaps through the window and flees into the night. Naturally I have no desire to be wounded in this altercation and I immediately throw the covers over my head and lie there while this cat fight rages up and down my frame with their sharp claws digging into my epidermis through the covers and the noise of the caterwauling sounding like two fire sirens blowing in the room. I stay covered up while they fight up and down the bed and off onto the floor, and then one of them, I don't know which, leaps through the window and the other one follows and I hear the noise of the fight still raging across the yard and through the shrubbery and down into the woods. How does Midnight look today?"

"He looks terrible," I said. "How does Pansy look?"

"I haven't seen him," she said. "But from the amount of fur left around, he must look awful, too."

So that is why Midnight cannot be in the play, *Alice in Wonderland,* at the Erlanger on the nights of March 20, 21, and 22. He may look all right by that time, but I do not feel like trusting him, now that he has turned out to be such a ruffian, jumping into people's windows to fight their cats. He might suddenly think about Pansy and fly into such a rage he would send poor Alice screaming from the stage in tears, all scratched up.

The Case of the Bridge-Player's Cat

I do not vouch for this story. In fact, it is almost too good a story to be true. It sounds like one of those stories that go around and you can always find somebody who knows somebody who saw it happen but you can never pin it down, and the first thing you know you have chased it right out of town to Birmingham, or somewhere.

But I have it on the word of Miss Winifred Rothermel, whom you may know as Miss Sally Saver, the food editor, and since it is about food, in a matter of speaking, I know Miss Saver would not deliberately delude me in the matter.

But to get on with it, as Miss Saver had it from a friend of hers, a woman of great probity, who merely told it as an amazing thing which happened to a neighbor of hers, without seeing anything funny in it.

It seems that this neighbor of Miss Saver's friend was having a group of the girls in one afternoon not long ago to knock off a few hands of bridge to bolster their morale, and since bridge is very fatiguing and nourishment is needed along toward the middle of the afternoon so the ladies may keep their strength up, she had prepared for her guests some tasty little sandwiches, made of sardines, and bits of salmon, and whatnot.

And it also seems that while she was dummy once, she slipped back into the kitchen to see if all was well with the sandwiches to find to her great distress that the family cat had gotten onto the table where the sandwiches were and had munched several of them while nobody was around to say her nay, or scat.

So the lady dips into the bowl where she has placed the remains of the salmon and whatnot and smears a few more bits of bread with the stuff and replaces the sandwiches which the cat had munched.

She then flings the cat into the backyard, with harsh words and imprecations, and goes on back to deal a few, saying nothing to her guests, of course, about the nefarious activities of the cat.

So all that afternoon she and her guests munch happily upon the sandwiches and she gets many compliments from her girl friends for how delicious they are.

Imagine then her consternation when, after the girls are gone and she goes out on the back porch to empty the ashtrays into the garbage can, she finds lying there the family cat, cold and stiff in death, with rigor mortis already in charge.

She is shocked and bewildered, of course, and immediately the horrible thought flashes through her mind that the cat has become poisoned by eating the salmon sandwiches.

So she hurries to the telephone and calls the family doctor and pours into his ear the full story of what has taken place and he admits that it does sound, indeed, as if the cat has died of eating the salmon sandwiches, a cat being admittedly careful to preserve its own life from all and sundry dangers except something insidious and unseen, like poison.

And he suggests that to be on the safe side he thinks that

she should call up the other girls and they should all come down to his office and he will meet them there and give them a good going over with his stomach pump.

So she calls up all the other girls and asks them how they are feeling, and they say they are feeling fine and why does she ask? And she tells them what has happened to the cat and they immediagely begin to feel strange pangs of pain, and there is a great screeching and gabbling going on over the phones. So they all rush down to the doctor's office, two tables of them, as Miss Saver recalls, and there the doctor works upon them most vigorously with the stomach pump.

As everybody knows this is one of the most unpleasant bits of medical treatment known to the profession, involving the swallowing of a hose which is only slightly smaller than a garden hose.

So, mere hollow shells of their former selves, they stagger weakly home. And our hostess, upon arriving at her domicile, flings herself down upon a sofa, becomes all unstrung and begins to sob bitterly at all the furor she has caused.

She is lying there sobbing, it seems, when the door opens gently and her neighbor from across the street comes tip-toeing in.

"Ah, my dear," she says, with tenderest sympathy. "I knew that I would find you prostrate with grief. But I just wanted to tell you that I was looking out the window this afternoon and I saw that car hit your cat—"

Cured for the Time, Anyway

I don't know whether the cure will be permanent or not, but for the moment at least I think I have solved the problem of my children's smoking cigarettes. What happened was this: I walked out on the porch at the mountain the other afternoon when my young evidently thought I was busy pecking on the typewriter on the back porch, and there were my two oldest and two of their little cousins perched up on the rail of the porch like a row of English sparrows. Each one of them had a lighted cigarette pinched between the thumb and forefinger in the manner in which people hold cigarettes when they are not used to smoking, and they were taking little puffs on the cigarettes and evidently thought they were looking very grown-up and sophisticated.

Naturally, the sight upset me, for no matter how much a man is addicted to nicotine himself, he does not like to see his children take up the habit. But he is on a spot. If he forbids them to smoke, it does not carry much weight, for he smokes, and they do not see why they can't do what he does. So they will sneak off and hide and smoke anyway. And if he tries to reason with them about smoking, telling them that it is bad for them and will stunt their growth, this does not have much effect, either. There is just no way a man can reasonably expect his children to refrain from acquiring the bad habits which he himself flaunts before them constantly.

So, rightly or wrongly, I tried another tack.

"Well, well," I said, with spurious amiability. "Here are all the young folks gathered together smoking cigarettes. That is fine. I am so glad to see you are growing up so fast. But for goodness sake, do not smoke in such a sissy and awkward manner. People will think that you do not know how to smoke. Now, you just watch me and I will show you."

So I took out a cigarette and lit it.

"Now," I said, "take a deep drag on your cigarette. Get a big mouthful of smoke."

Looking a little dubious, they took a deep puff on their cigarettes.

"Now," I said, "breathe in deep, taking the smoke deep down into your lungs. And then blow it out slowly, through your nose."

They knew by this time they were in for trouble, but they made a brave effort. They took a deep breath of smoke and tried to blow it out through their noses, and you never heard such coughing and wheezing and carrying on. Their eyes were watering and the taste of smoke was terrible in their mouths, and they were trying to throw the cigarettes away and escape.

But I was very firm with them.

"No," I said. "People do not just take a couple of drags and then throw the cigarette away. That is very wasteful of the fine mellow tobacco which the tobacco people put in these cigarettes. We all are going to smoke our cigarettes right down to a stub. Now, take another deep drag, and then another and another and another, and then we will all light fresh cigarettes and take up the pleasant art of blowing smoke rings."

But they never did get around to blowing smoke rings. By the time I made them take about six puffs, inhaling each, they were not only suffering from the smoke getting in their eyes and noses, making their eyes water, but one of them was actually crying, begging to be allowed to throw his cigarette away, and all of them were beginning to look greenish around the jaw line, and their faces were the color of a tallow candle.

Finally, they could stand it no longer. The one in the worst shape threw his cigarette down and lurched off the porch, seeking some place to lie down and expire quietly, and the others followed suit, all of them very rocky on their pins and extremely upset, mentally and otherwise.

And now they are all a little angry with me, but I think there is a strong possibility that they will not take up the smoking of cigarettes again soon, if ever. In fact, they will not even stay around when I am smoking, if the wind is blowing the smoke in their direction.

When Blue Jay Fails to Notice Cat, Spring Is Here

The other morning I went out and swept some of the slushy snow off the table on the terrace and put out the birdseed and went back into the house and waited. Pretty soon the birds came in—doves mostly, and little jerky-tailed sparrows, and a female towhee, and finally a blue jay. But the jay didn't seem to have his mind on feeding. He pecked away a couple of times and then I saw him straighten up and put his head on one side as if he were listening. Then he flew up in the little water oak that stands by the terrace, and faintly, through the closed window, I heard those beautiful two-note calls that a blue jay makes when there is something on his mind other than screaming angrily and calling somebody "a thief."

So I went back to the kitchen and eased the door open so I could hear what was going on; and the blue jay in the water oak called again, that same sweet soft musical whistle; and from far down in the woods came an answer, just as soft, just as sweet, just as musical.

About this time I saw, coming across the snowy yard, picking his feet up high and putting them down, the biggest smoke-gray tomcat you ever saw, a real old tiger of a tomcat. He came sneaking across the open yard, and under the tree where the jay sang, and I said to myself, Thomas, you are in for trouble. As soon as that jay sees you he is going to come down out of that tree like a blue streak of lightning and he is going to pluck hairs out of your tail until you go out of sight under the hydrangea bush. You will have a tail peeled bare as a possum's tail before he is through with you.

But you know what that silly, lovesick, spring-struck jaybird did? He sat there singing that single love note while the tomcat passed unnoticed right under him. And if I hadn't rushed out there yelling scat and throwing snowballs, that cat would have caught a feeding sparrow right before my eyes.

It just goes to show, I guess, that snow or no snow, winter is nearly over. When the blue jays start feeling so romantic they can't see a prowling tomcat right under their noses, spring can't be far behind.

Everybody Was Glad Except the Cat

The black cat, Captain Midnight, who is more or less in charge around my house in my absence, it seems, is none too well pleased that I am back home.

It appears that while I was away he got in the habit of coming in soon after he had his dinner, curling up in my chair and slumbering there for the remainder of the evening. If anybody wanted to sit there, they had to pick him up bodily and put him on the floor; but they didn't get any pleasure out of the chair, because he would go under it, where he couldn't be reached, and express his displeasure by reaching out and sticking a barbed claw, evidently made of steel, into their ankles. When I came back and bounced him out of the chair, he pulled that stunt on me and we had words about the matter. Then, when I got up to go put some antiseptic on the lacerated ankle, he got back in the chair again.

What happened then, the kids say, was an accident, but I don't know. I think I was booby-trapped. Anyway, I noticed that one of the youngsters had thrown his coat in the seat of the chair, but being angry at the moment I did not move the coat but just sat down on it and the cat, it seems, was under it, lying in ambush. Well, I still bear the marks of that one, and that time I not only threw the cat out of the chair, I threw him out of the house.

It was a cold night, and somebody went and let him in without my knowledge, and he went back and got on my bed, another habit acquired while I was gone. So when I went back to go to bed, there he was, and I chased him off and he went out, yowling angrily.

But I ignored his protests, and went in and ran some water in the tub and turned it off when there was enough and went back into the bedroom for something; and as I started back into the bathroom, here comes the cat racing out. He was soaking wet all over, and he went tearing down the hall and into the living room, scattering water all over the wallpaper and uttering loud, harsh cries of anger and distress.

So now I am being accused of playing a dirty trick on the cat. For the kids say I knew that when the cat wanted a drink of water he just hopped over into the tub and drank from the water that collects under the faucet, which drips all the time. And they think I ran some water in the tub knowing that the cat would jump in, not knowing the tub was full, and frighten himself out of his wits, and they think it is a skunk trick and anybody who would play such a trick is a louse. And if I didn't do it as a trick, why did I fill the tub instead of taking a shower, as always? And anyway, why was it cold water?

Well, I am not going to try to argue the matter with them because I stand convicted, as I can plainly see. But I bet that cat does not try to push me around any more. I bet he knows who is the master of the house now.

Though I can easily understand how he was not as glad to see me as were the human members of my household, something was said the other day that made me wonder a little just how genuine was their welcome. A friend whose family is away was riding home with us and he happened to observe:

"You really do miss your folks when they are out of town."

To which my smallest son made a statement that amused everybody. Everybody but me:

"When Daddy's out of town," he said, "we miss the car."

Only Captain Midnight Missing Upon Return From Far Pacific

Things were rocking along in their normal confusion when I came home the other evening after a sojourn in other parts which lasted considerably longer than suited me. The cook had caught her thumb in the ironing machine, mashing it somewhat, which surprised me a little, for I would have expected her to get caught in the washing machine, if she got caught in anything. She also was complaining about the New Long Look, which she feels she has not been able to achieve to the extent that she would like. Since she stands about five feet four and weighs 190 pounds, being about as broad as a bale of cotton, I can understand that the New Long Look does present some problems, but I didn't say so. There is no sense in annoying a good cook in this day and time.

Some old things were missing, and a few new things had showed up during the six months of my absence. An ancient suit which I dearly loved, since it hung upon me like a burlap bag, completely comfortable, was gone, and when I started making inquiries about it, the women in my household muttered something about burglars, or it must be around somewhere, and asking each other if anybody remembered where they saw it last, but they can't fool me. I know what they did. As soon as I got out of town they gave it away to the garbage man or somebody. And it was a good suit, too. I bought it just before I was married twelve years ago, and I had become attached to it. A lot of other things, such as chewing gum, had become attached to it also, and I'm afraid that has something to do with its disappearance.

My old friend, Dr. Hoppy, the white rabbit, was missing also. He is now living happily out at Fernbank Children's Zoo with a lot of other rabbits of the opposite sex, and I am sure he is happy there. It seems that shortly after I left, the dog down the street, a big bulldog named Fronto Creighton-Toombs, caught Dr. Hoppy out behind the scuppernong vine and almost scalped him, peeling all the skin off his nose and frightening him so that when my wife rescued him he lay in a state of shock for the better part of a day. Knowing that she would either have to shoot Fronto Creighton-Toombs, which would probably offend his owner, or give away Dr. Hoppy, she took him out to Fernbank and put him in the zoo, where he seems to be very happy. The children go out to see him sometimes, but he does not pay much attention to them. He hops up to the cage and wiggles his nose at them and eats whatever they bring, but they say there is no light of recognition in his eyes, and he soon hops off about his own affairs. He is a man of family now and seems to have no memory of his first home, nor any desire to return to it. I can't blame him much, for he spent most of his time indoors being lugged around by the ears, like a suitcase, and most of the time he was outdoors he was scampering madly through the brush with Fronto Creighton-Toombs bellowing furiously at his heels.

The thing that really distressed me, though, was to come home to find Captain Midnight gone. Nobody knows where he went. He just went away one night and didn't come back. Knowing him as an old roisterer and roué at heart, I am not too much worried about his safety, though some of my household fear that he met with foul play. I think he just got bored and went out to see the world. I wouldn't be surprised to see him come swaggering up the walk some night with that arrogant look of his. If he does, I want to be there; for the fur is going to fly. His place has been taken by a big fat oafish cat named Chester, Jr., (I must remember to ask who Chester, Sr., was), who lies around snoozing all day and, so far as I know, never howled to the moon from a back fence in his life, a sport that old Midnight dearly loved. They say that Chester, Jr., is a fine, sweet-tempered cat, and that I am wrong in calling him a dolt, but I don't know. I like a cat that moves around with a chip on his shoulder, like old Midnight. And I'll bet that if Midnight ever does come back and finds Chester there, he'll put Chester up the chimney raked with clawmarks from stem to stern.

It may seem strange to thoughtful readers that a man will go off and wander around the world for six months and then come home to write trivia about cats and old suits and white rabbits. But to tell you the truth, that's all I want to think about for a while—about kids and cats and the simple things of home.

There's only one conclusion that any traveler can draw about the state of the world at present—and that is that things are in one hell of a bad shape everywhere. There is nothing but distrust and fear wherever you go—with all the world looking to us—to the United States, I mean—to find the answers to their troubles, economic and political.

And I don't know what those answers are, and there's no use pretending that I do.

To Get Rid of Spiders, Shake Their Ears Off

Little Miss Muffett has been avenged. I went into the bathroom the other morning and there was a small brown spider sitting on the handle of my electric toothbrush—not on the handle post that contains the vibrating machinery, but the little short plastic handle which you push down into the vibrator.

So I very carefully took the toothbrush out of its plastic holder, being careful not to disturb the spider, and plugged it into the vibrator, and pushed the button and the toothbrush started vibrating . . . bzzzz . . . about a million times a minute.

Well, the Humane Society may get after me about this, but if you ever saw anything funny in your life, it is a spider trying to hold onto an electric toothbrush when it's vibrating. I don't know how many legs a spider has, but he was using them all, clinging on for dear life, and it was buzzing so fast he was just a blur and his little red eyes were about to pop out. You could tell he was getting addled. He'd run up and down the toothbrush handle trying to find some way to turn loose, but he couldn't let go.

Finally, I got sorry for him, and pushed the button to

stop the vibrating. He sat there for a moment waiting for his head to clear, I suppose. Then he gave one huge leap off into space, floated to the floor on an invisible filament, and the last I saw of him he was scooting through the crack under the door, headed for the great outdoors.

I have been watching for him, but so far as I know he hasn't been back since.

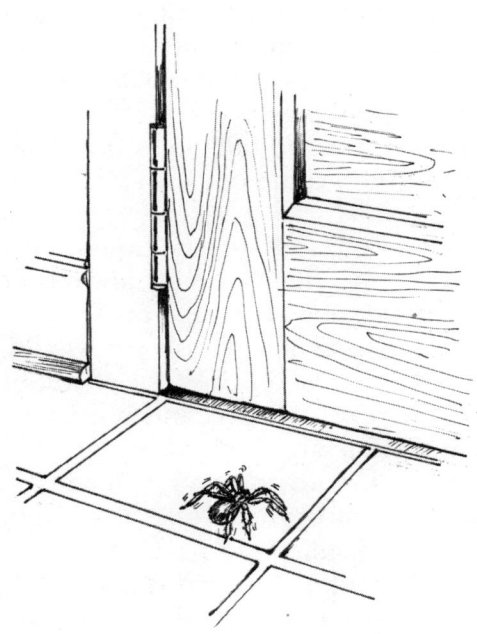

The Wily Ways of Our Progeny

What I am trying to figure out is, have I been outsmarted or not? I have been brooding over the matter for some days now, and I have about come to the conclusion the answer is "Yes." It began with one of those offhanded requests. You know the kind, when they come climbing up in your lap and sort of snuggle up and talk about nothing in particular for a minute and then come out with what is really on their minds.

This time it was: "Daddy, every time I go to spend the night with one of my friends almost always they have a cat and it is the cutest thing. It sleeps on the foot of our bed and goes 'zzzzz zzzz zzzz' and I wish you would get me a cat to play with and to sleep on the foot of my bed."

Well, I am a very softhearted and indulgent parent, and strive to give my offspring all the things that will make their little hearts leap up with joy and I am just about to say, "Why, yes, darling, you can have a cat," when I remember the last cat we had, a sullen old harridan named Minnie the Moocher, which wouldn't sleep on any bed but mine and suffered from asthma and made the night hideous with her snoring. Plus being stubborn and surly of temper, so that when I tried to pick her up and throw her off the bed she would sink her claws into the blanket and hang on, sometimes sinking her claws also into my epidermis with the result that there was a great battle there in the middle of the night between me and Minnie the Moocher, always ending up with me out of the bed, trying to gather up the covers and get them straightened out, with Minnie lying there wheezing triumphantly, still unevicted from my sack.

So I say, "No, we do not need a cat around this house," and she slides down off my lap with a peculiar gleam in her eye.

But the next night the formula is repeated, except this time I almost leap out of my chair, for what she asks for is a horse.

"Daddy," she says, "I have been thinking about what I would like so much for my birthday and I want you to get me a horse, because I love horses so much and I have already got my jodhpurs and boots and if we had a horse I could ride every day instead of just when I go out to Fritz's and it is the most fun and . . . ."

"Whoa," I say, firmly, knowing that here was something that must be nipped in the bud or there is no telling what tears and recriminations are liable to follow. "Horses," I say, "cost a lot of money. You cannot just go downtown and buy a horse like you buy a handkerchief. And we do not have a place to keep a horse, anyway."

"I know a lot about horses," she said. "They do not lie down to sleep at night so you do not have to have a bed for them. We could let the horse stay out under the oak tree in the backyard."

"Horses," I said, "do not like to stand up under oak trees in backyards all night. They like to have stables to stay in, and the way things are around this house, with children sleeping in the dining room, I am not going to build any accommodations for a horse. If I build anything else around this house, it is going to be a place for children to sleep, not horses. Anyway, we do not have anything to feed a horse."

"I thought about that," she said. "And I know what we can do. You know how we hate to cut the lawn. Well, we can let the horse eat the grass on the lawn, and you will not have to cut it."

"Listen," I said. "You know that there is not enough grass on our lawn to keep an eohippus in good nourishment, and the eohippus was the primitive ancestor of the horse and stood only six inches high at the shoulder. Now go away and do not bother me any more about a horse."

But she returned to the attack night after night. With pictures of horses torn from magazines. With books about horses. Even with some of those little white horses that come off of bottles of imported spirits, though where she got those in this day and time I do not know. She saw some bronze statues of a horse, a mare and a colt in a jeweler's window, and she took out after me about buying her these statues, though they cost nine dollars apiece.

Finally, I had a bright idea. "Look, beautiful," I said, "I tell you what would be nicer than a horse. We could get a cat. You do not have to build a stable for a cat. . . ."

She leaped down out of my lap with a shriek of delight and went tearing out of the room. "Mommy," she was yelling. "Isn't it WONDERFUL? Daddy says we can have a cat."

Just about that time a great light began to dawn on me. I am glad she didn't campaign for an elephant, or a camel, or a Peruvian llama. I might have compromised on a horse.

A Rooster Trio Crows at Dawn

A few weeks ago in a rash moment I wrote in this space that one thing I missed after living in the city all these years was hearing a rooster crow. Well, this morning just at daylight I heard a rooster crow. He crowed in my backyard. He reared back and crowed until the leaves trembled on the trees and the dog woke up and the cat sprang from the foot of my bed and looked about wildly.

Being a city cat, he had never heard such a noise before and it left him somewhat unstrung.

It left me unstrung, too. I do not own any roosters. I do not know anybody who owns roosters. So it was obvious to me that the dog, the cat, and I were all the simultaneous victims of some kind of illusion. If there can be optical illusions which deceive the eye, I figured, there can also be audio illusions which deceive the ear. Particularly at five o'clock in the morning when dogs, cats, and men alike are dazed and drugged with sleep. So I turned over and went back to sleep.

And I did not think anything more about this strange thing until at breakfast time I happened to mention that I had had a most peculiar dream. I had dreamed I heard a rooster crowing.

HAROLD MARTIN REMEMBERS

"Dream, heck," my son said. "I've got news for you. You did hear a rooster crow. This morning I'm asleep, see, and I hear this big noise, 'Karook aroooooo,' and I look out the window and there is a big brown-colored rooster standing in the backyard crowing. Then I look again and two more roosters walk up and they all crow and then they walk down into the woods together."

So I brood over this all day until late in the afternoon when the phone rings and a nice lady-like voice asks me did the chickens arrive all right.

And I said they sure did, they arrived in full voice about five o'clock, and who was this? And she said she was just a friend of mine, the name didn't matter and she was so glad about the roosters. She dropped them off at my house about eleven o'clock the night before and she just knew I would enjoy them so much. She enjoyed them herself and hated to give them up. But the neighbors got to fussing, she said, and threatening to call the police. So she just thought she'd surprise me—and please me—by bringing them over to my house.

I think that was mighty nice of her.

And I'm sorry she didn't give me her name. I am going to Florida next week and I would like to bring her a nice present—an alligator, maybe. Or a small crocodile.

"Bub" Not So Bad, After All

Years ago, before I became a family man, I decided that if any of my offspring, in case there should be any, ever addressed me with flippant mock respect as "pater," I would take them out behind the barn and give them a going over with a hickory switch.

The way things have turned out, I think I would be glad to settle for "pater." The things I have been called lately have set me to foaming slightly. I was sitting there the other day, peacefully smoking my pipe and perusing a good book when my daughter came bouncing in from school.

"Howdy, Bub," she said, in a high, cracked voice that was vaguely reminiscent of somebody I had heard on the radio. She bounced on upstairs.

"Come back here," I shouted. She came back and stood in the door, very formally.

"Did your highness call?" she said, like an English butler in a costume play, seeking to ascertain the wishes of some bumbling earl.

"I did," I said, "I called to inform you that my name is not 'Bub.' I am your father, a person considerably older than you—old enough, I trust, to be accorded some respect around this house. . . ."

"Well, bless your little pointed head," she said, patting me on it. "I did not dream you would take offense. . . ."

"Listen," I said, "what is this about somebody's little pointed head. Do not be referring to me in any such disrespectful manner. Think of the younger children. How can I advise and counsel them and subject them to the normal discipline which a parent should exercise when a flippant little flibbertigibbet. . . ."

"That's a good word," she said, "flippant little flipperti . . . what was the rest of it? I must remember to tell Chumley. . . ."

"Never mind, " I said sternly. "Just do not be so casual in the future when you speak to your elders."

"I'm sorry," she said, looking as if she were. "I won't do it again, pops." She started out and paused. "Pops," she said, questioningly, "that's all right, isn't it? That's kind of a cozy word."

"It's all right, I guess," I said, "for around the house. Don't use it outside, though. It sounds too much as if I am fat and bald and. . . ."

"You will be," she said.

"What's that?" I said, "what was that scurrilous remark?"

"What does squirrelous mean?" she said.

"Never mind about that," I said. "Goodbye."

"So long," she said, scooting upstairs.

Well, I thought, that was that. Maybe from now on I would be accorded a little bit more respect around my house. A man has to draw the line somewhere. He cannot let things get out of hand. "Howdy, Bub," indeed! There would be no more of that.

The next afternoon I was sitting there in the chair and the door banged and here she came, scooting through the room headed for the stairs. She did not see me.

"Good afternoon," I said, politely from my corner. "Did you have a nice day at school?"

She stopped short and turned.

"Hi yah, love-child," she said. "Sure I had a swell day. . . . What's the matter? You are all red. Is your collar choking you?"

"No," I said, feebly. "No, my collar is not choking me . . . goodbye."

"Bye," she said.

I sat there for a long time, thinking. She came back down the stairs.

"From now on," I said, knowing when I was beaten, "just make it Bub. I guess that will be all right."

Let the Doctor Explain the Mysteries of Manhood

He came into the kitchen to fix himself a sandwich and there was nobody in the house but him and me, so I figured now was as good a time as any.

"Look," I said, "your mama thinks I ought to have a talk with you. She thinks maybe there are some things I ought to tell you. . . ."

"About what?" he said, spreading mayonnaise on a piece of bread.

"Well," I said. "About lots of things. About girls. . . ."

"What about girls?" he said. His voice was low and deep on the "what" but it kind of broke in the middle and squeaked when he got to "girls."

"Well," I said. "There are lots of things maybe you ought to know. I have noticed here lately that your voice is beginning to change. It is not a small boy's voice all the time any more but is getting deep and husky like a man. . . ."

He put a couple of slices of ham on the bread, put a top on it, and took a big bite.

"Whaf my voif god do wuf gurfs?" he said.

"Dont' talk with your mouth full," I said. "The fact that your voice is changing has got a lot to do with girls. It

CATS AND DOGS, CHILDREN AND OTHER SMALL CREATURES

means your whole . . . well . . . your whole point of view is changing. . . ."

"How?" he said, taking another bite of the sandwich.

"Look," I said, "don't ask me questions. Just shut up and let me talk. It means that you are growing up and are beginning to think about things that small boys don't think of much because they are too busy playing cowboys and looking at television, and riding bicycles and. . . ."

"Wha' kina things?" he said.

"All sorts of things," I said. "Like, well, like thinking maybe some girl you never paid any attention to before is very pretty and sweet, and you feel like you would like to hold her hand and maybe kiss her and . . . and . . . well, and a lot of other things like that. . . . Don't back me into a corner . . . you know what I'm trying to. . . ."

He finished the sandwich and wiped the crumbs off his chin with his hand and wiped his hand on the front of his shirt.

"Look, Pop, isn't this a little embarrassing to you?" he said.

"Well," I said. "Yes. I guess it is, at that."

"Me too," he said. "Let's go see what's on the television."

So that's the way it turned out and I guess I didn't do much of a job of telling my son about the facts of life. And now, I discover, if I had waited I could have saved myself a lot of trouble. For at the office the other morning there arrives a small book from the presses of Tupper and Love. It is called *For Boys Only* and it is written by a doctor named Frank Howard Richardson who lives in North Carolina. He is a distinguished physician with three sons of his own, and in plain, simple words he puts down all the answers to the questions that a teenage boy might ask his father if he weren't too embarrassed to ask, and it tells a boy all that a father would like for him to know.

And for anybody in my position, with a son he'd like to talk to about certain very important things which may mean the difference in him growing up to be the kind of man people like and respect, or a jerk, it's a good book. It talks a little about smoking and drinking and driving a car like a screwball, but mostly it talks about what happens, physically and emotionally, in that strange time when the voice is beginning to deepen and down appears on the upper lip, and girls are suddenly beautiful and fascinating.

The subtitle to it is "The Doctor Discusses the Mysteries of Manhood" and I know what I'm going to do. I'm going to take it home and put it on his desk without saying anything. And after he reads it, if there are any questions he wants to ask, I'll try to answer them. But I don't think there will be. The doctor answers them all.

He Can't Keep From Brawling

I had fondly thought that as my cat, Chester, Jr., came into the fullness of his years he would mend his ways and become a respectable citizen of the community. I figured that sooner or later he would fling his last wild oat to the winds of a raffish world and curl up by the fireside to doze his days and nights away, an example to the young cats of the neighborhood. It looks as if the time is not yet. After a month or so of conduct circumspect as that of any deacon, old Chester broke over again this week. He fell off the wagon, I am positive, and whatever else he was up to, I do not allow myself to dwell upon.

At any rate, the moonlit night was ringing with his mellow baritone in what sounded suspiciously like a quartet gathered back in the shower-bath room of a barbershop on Saturday night after the blinds have been drawn. And after the quartet singing was over there was a great deal more singing—duet singing in which a fine soprano, very strong and sure in the upper ranges, was heard.

As such evenings often do, this one ended up in one whale of a brannigan, and where for hours the air had been mellow with the feline version of "Sweet Adeline," "Drink to

HAROLD MARTIN REMEMBERS

Me Only With Thine Eyes" and "There Was an Old Ship on the Sandy Seashore," shrieks and howls of rage and anguish filled the air. I thought for a while I should go out and try to act as peacemaker, but I happened to recall one unfortunate instance when I played that role among certain of my human acquaintances, and had to go home in an overcoat borrowed from a waiter, having lost all but the waistband to a pair of tuxedo pants.

So, I figured if Chester was going to have his fun, like the rest of us, he'd have to pay for it. I didn't realize, though, just how much it was costing him. When I went to the back door to let him in the next morning he was so badly beaten up he didn't even speak in his usual insouciant manner. He just staggered in, meowing faintly, and headed for the bathtub to get a drink of water. He had three long scratches beginning right under his left eye and going all the way down to his nose, two or three whiskers had been pulled out by the roots, and there was a big gash in his right ear. I don't know what the other cat looked like, but if Chester won that brawl, his foe must be a sorry sight.

Ordinarily, when Chester is drinking water from the leaky faucet in the tub and I stick my head in, he leaps from the tub and flees down the hall. In trying to help him once I turned the upper row of handles instead of the lower, and scalded Chester in a sudden burst of hot water from the shower and he hasn't trusted me since. This time, though, he just sat there, meowing, while I turned the water on just a trickle so he could drink, and he lapped at the falling water for about ten minutes. He was really dehydrated.

When he finally leaped painfully out of the tub, I took him into the living room and gave him a good talking to about how unseemly his conduct had been for a cat of his age. He seemed to be truly penitent.

But I don't know . . . I've seen him in these moods of repentance before, and they never lasted long. Comes a night when a full moon shines and the voices of his bad companions float high and clear upon the air, and the first thing I know he is at the back door yowling to be let out. The old gleam is in his eye, and he carries his tail like a plume.

The old boy tries hard to be good, I know. But the flesh is weak, and I sadly fear he'll be a rounder all his days.

Mr. McGill Joins the Fancy

I am disturbed to discover that Mr. Ralph McGill, my boss and good friend of long standing, has now joined the ranks of those who hold the house cat in high esteem. For many years, in fact ever since I have known him, Mr. McGill has looked with disdain upon cats. He was a dog man since infancy, raised with puppies, and he had a tendency to look upon a man who was fond of cats as being slightly suspect. There was, he seemed to convey, something sissy about a man who liked cats, a faint streak of lavender. In fact, I have ofttimes had my feelings hurt by Mr. McGilll in regard to cats. I would come to the office bubbling over with enthusiasm about some exploit of my cat, Chester, Jr., and Mr. McGill would yawn right in the middle of my discourse and turn back to his typewriter. He would treat Chester rudely when he came to my house to visit. Chester is very fond of jumping up on beds and getting his rest there, and Mr. McGill's vest, when he sits down, has an expanse roughly that of a double bed. So Chester would jump upon Mr. McGill's lap and attempt to curl up there and get his rest, and Mr. McGill would seize Chester by the scruff of his neck and toss him across the room.

CATS AND DOGS, CHILDREN AND OTHER SMALL CREATURES

Chester would purr and attempt to rub himself against Mr. McGill's leg, and Mr. McGill would nudge him in the ribs with such violence that Chester would sail through the air like a football. It made for a certain amount of strain between us, but being in the employ of Mr. McGill, I could not rebuke him for kicking my cat.

And now Mr. McGill himself has succumbed to the cat fever. He went on a fishing trip down to Florida some time ago, and there he made the acquaintance of a large yellow Manx cat which hung around the docks where the fishing boats came in. He said this cat was in charge of the dock. Dogs would approach the cat and the cat would take out after them and chase them so far into the Everglades that nobody ever saw them again except the Seminoles.

He said this cat was such a gallant cat that all the kittens in that part of Florida had the same stub tails and the same arrogant swagger. Mr. McGill became a member, in spirit, of the fancy. He wrote a most enthralling piece about this cat and expressed the wish that he had a similar cat.

And then the cats began to arrive. A lady sent Mr. McGill a small black cat which was not a pure Manx cat but it carried its backside way up in the air like a rabbit, and it had a stub tail, indicating that its great-great-great-grandfather was probably a Manx cat. And then another lady wrote Mr. McGill that she was sending him a cream-colored Manx kitten that was of such noble ancestry that it had no tail at all. She was going to enter this kitten in the cat show down at the auditorium November 25 and 26, and after the show she was presenting this kitten to Mr. McGill.

And now Mr. McGill has become so fond of cats that I expect him to start picking his cat up and cuddling it, and talking baby talk to it, like the ladies at the cat show do with their cats. He comes into the office in the morning to report that this black cat at his house is the smartest cat he ever saw.

He talks at great length about this cat, and to repay him

for past unkindnesses I yawn in the middle of his discourse and turn back to my typewriter. But he is just like all cat folks. He does not seem to notice that you are not interested in the exploits of his cat.

Mr. McGill is particularly interested in the Manx cat. He thinks the Manx cat is the greatest fighting cat there is. The Manx cat is a tough cat, he says, that swam ashore to the Isle of Man when the Spanish Armada was wrecked. He says the Manx cat was tougher than the Spanish sailors, because the sailors did not swim ashore, but the cats did.

I do not resent the fact that Mr. McGill has become fond of cats. But I am a little disturbed about his entering his cat in the cat show in competition with my cat, Chester, Jr. If he goes swaggering around down there bragging about what a fighting cat his cat is, my cat Chester is going to take umbrage at this, and the first time he catches Mr. McGill's Manx cat out he is going to maul Mr. McGill's cat severely.

There is nothing in the journalism book that says what a newspaperman should do if his cat whips the editor's cat, but if Mr. McGill is truly imbued with the affection for his cat that most cat owners feel for their felines, there is going to be trouble. I have seen ladies at the cat show get huffy with each other just because one of them had a cat that went "phhhhtttt" at the other one's cat. They would glare at each other through their spectacles and breathe heavily through their noses. I am afraid if my cat whips Mr. McGill's cat, it may have a disastrous effect on my career in journalism. We will just have to wait and see.

Wherever He Is, Smokey Deserves the Best

Smokey, the big shambling, half hound, half collie who lived down the street, disappeared about three weeks ago, and everybody in the neighborhood is missing him.

Smokey nominally belonged to the Alfred Thompsons, down on Argonne. They fed him, and gave him a place to sleep, and bought his collars, and got him his rabies shots, and took him to the vet when he was feeling poorly.

But actually, Smokey was everybody's dog. He kept watch on all the houses, and looked after all the children. He would make the rounds in the morning just to see that the kids got off to school all right, and when school was out in the afternoon, he'd come back to watch them at their play. Sometimes, at night, when we'd come in late from a party, there'd be old Smokey, sitting at the back door, waiting to welcome us home. He seemed to know when a house was empty, and needed watching.

He collected a small fee for these services, of course. He'd eat out of every dog's bowl along the street, and drink the milk put out for the cats. And the funny thing about it was, the dogs didn't seem to mind old Smokey's mooching. They seemed to understand that he was a kind of canine elder statesman, keeping order in the community, and they didn't even growl at him when he came around.

I think what Smokey was looking for mainly, on his visits around the community, was loving. He wanted somebody to scratch him behind the ears, and everybody did. I'd be sitting out on the back terrace on a summer evening, listening to the night, when all of a sudden I'd feel a cold nose nudging at my hand, and there'd be old Smokey, wanting to be scratched. When he'd see me out in the yard, raking leaves, he'd come and lie down, right in front of me, rolling over on his back, so I could scratch him with the leaf rake. One night, I remember, we were sitting out in the backyard in the dark, when Smokey came up suddenly, and put his head in Mama's lap, not knowing that my old tomcat, Captain Midnight, was asleep in Mama's lap. Well, Midnight gave Smokey one swipe across the nose with his claws, then he jumped and lit right on top of Mama's head, standing there with his back arched and his tail buzzed up, digging his claws into her coiffure. I still think it was the funniest thing I ever saw, Mama sitting there with that cat on her head.

Smokey hated water worse than any dog I ever saw. He couldn't stand a shower of rain. I remember once, when it was raining pretty hard, he took refuge under the little overhang at my kitchen door. About that time Mama drove up, and started to get out of the car with an armload of groceries. The minute she opened the car door old Smokey lunged for it, knocking her back into the car. I looked out and there was Mama with groceries scattered everywhere, with Smokey sitting in her lap in the front seat of the car. She shoved him out and he jumped right back in. She dragged him out by the collar, and he was back in before she could get the door shut. She was the wettest, maddest lady I ever saw before she finally slammed the car door, stalked over to the kitchen door and started in. Wham! Old Smokey hit the door running, and there went Mama and the groceries again.

CATS AND DOGS, CHILDREN AND OTHER SMALL CREATURES

I used to pull a mean trick on old Smokey. In the summertime, when the family, and my dog Shim, were up in the mountains, the house would get full of fleas. So I'd invite old Smokey in, and walk him around over the house, until he'd collected all the fleas. He never seemed to mind. I guess he figured he had so may fleas already that a few more wouldn't hurt.

Alfred Thompson thinks somebody may have stolen Smokey. There's a rumor to the effect that people are stealing fine dogs in the neighborhood, and taking them to other states to sell, for several registered dogs are missing, and the pound declares they didn't pick them up. Smokey, of course, was no fine dog, though he looked like one. He had dignity, and he carried himself like a senator. And he had a kind and loving heart. And I hope that wherever he is, somebody is petting him, and scratching him behind the ears, and letting him come into the house every time it rains.

Mockingbirds Have a No-Cat Zone

It seems to be the consensus of the bird-watchers in the community that I goofed badly in this space last week. I told a lady that the mockingbirds in her yard would stop pulling the hair out of her cat's tail as soon as they had enough to line their nest. By letters and by telephone, the bird folks have been leaping to the attack.

Mockingbirds do not pull the hairs out of cats' tails because they wish to line their nest, they say. They pull them out because they cannot stand the sight of a cat and will not permit them to come anywhere near their nest.

One nice lady who has a mockingbird nest in her backyard gave me a complete description of the attitude of the mockingbird toward a neighbor's cat and the way it varied during the nest-building, egg-laying, hatching, and flying periods.

At first, she said, when the mockingbirds were building their nest they didn't pay any particular attention to the cat, which disproves my theory that mockingbirds like to line their nests with cat fur.

As soon as they got the nest built, though, and the mama bird started sitting on the eggs, the mama and papa birds drew an invisible line about forty feet from the tree across which no cat was permitted to pass. If he did, they would fly down, the two of them together, assaulting the cat both fore and aft, one of them pecking him on the head while the other one tweaked his tail.

This boundary lasted throughout the hatching season, the lady said. Then when the little birds began to feather out and started to try their wings, the birds greatly expanded the no-cat zone. Knowing that the youngsters would grow weary and flutter to the ground after a flight of some distance, they did not even permit the cat to leave his own house across the street. As soon as he would come out and sit on the front steps, washing his face, they would dart over there and rap on his skull and chase him all the way under the house.

Even people, the lady says, are not safe from mockingbirds when they think their fledglings are in danger. One morning her little boy went out, carrying the broom, to help the mockingbirds chase the cat away. They didn't want any help. They put the cat to flight and then turned around and chased her little boy into the house.

How to Drive a Parent Crazy

NEW YORK—They were coming down Fifth Avenue, and you could tell they were out-of-towners by the way they walked, because they looked, as they walked, into the show-windows of the stores, where gems glittered on blue plush, and upward to the top of the buildings. And when they came to the intersections they didn't just swivel their necks quickly to the right and left and then go on across, dodging through the traffic. They waited for the lights to change. People who live here don't walk the streets that way. They walk fast, and their eyes are far away and there is something on their minds and they do not pay any attention to the streets through which they walk, or to the people on the streets.

Anyway, here they went, down the street. A young couple about thirty-five maybe, papa tall, and mama short and blonde and quick-stepping. And papa was carrying in his arms a little boy about four years old, and mama had her arms full of packages. And in front of them, coursing the street like a puppy, darting ahead and then falling back, was a little guy about six years old, one of those bouncy little boys so full of life that he could not contain himself.

And all along the street they were worrying about the little fellow who was walking, and once in a while mama, at the great risk of dropping her packages, would grab for his hand and try to hold him and make him walk along quietly, but he wouldn't stay at her side. He kept breaking away.

And I walked along behind, watching them, and sympathizing with them, because he had them over the barrel and they were scared to death he was going to trip some of the hurrying crowd that was flowing from the other direction or get lost, and they kept calling to him to wait, or to come on, and he was paying no attention. He just kept scooting about, all bundled up in his heavy coat and his zipper pants, and his cap with the earmuffs down over his ears.

And they came up to the intersection, with him out front about fifteen feet going along at the heels of four men who were walking abreast. And the light was red, and the men, glancing quickly, darted across with the youngster right behind them, going against the light. And the taxi came wheeling around the corner and the little boy was right in front of it and the cabbie swerved. But the left front fender hit him and knocked him sprawling, and in that quick moment when it was hard to know whether he was going to live or die there rose from all around a cry of such terror and such agony as seldom I have ever heard. There was the high thin scream of the youngster's mother, and the noise his father made was like the sound a man would make if he tried to cry out while a hand clutched at his throat. It was a hoarse, choking cry and there were, from all around, the terrified shouts of the people who had suddenly seen the little fellow there in the middle of the street and the taxi bearing down on him.

The fender struck him, and knocked him off his feet, and he hit on his back and skidded along for a way in the icy slush of the street, and the crowd rushed to him and gathered around and somebody picked him up and held him in their arms.

And bless me if he didn't kick like a shoat, and scramble down out of the man's arms, and run on across the street and over to a window, where he put his nose up against the glass and blew his breath on the pane to make it misty, and then he took his finger and rubbed it zig-zag across the misty place.

Then he looked up and across the street to where his father and mother stood, still too limp with terror to move, and he yelled across the intersection, past the taxi driver who had hit him, who still sat in his cab, his face the color of yellow cheese:

"C'mon, Mama. Watcha just standin' there for?"

I was walking beside his father then, and his face was white and wet and he was trembling and he was saying over and over, "I'll break his neck, I'll break his neck. . . ."

But he didn't. He rushed across the street and dropped the other youngster, plunk, onto the slushy sidewalk on his bottom, and reached out for the little guy, and gathered him into his arms.

Peace Can Be Lonely, Too

Suddenly, the house felt still. While I was having my coffee, the first one—the biggest boy—came down, gulped his cereal and his egg, fixed himself his luncheon sandwich, and yelled "So long, Pop" from the kitchen door. I watched him through the window as he walked down the driveway to catch the bus for school, and marveled at the size of him, the height, the spread of shoulders. Was it only yesterday he came, redfaced and squalling, into the world? Outside a few minutes later a car horn blew and another one—the oldest girl—peered through the venetian blinds, gulped her milk, and rose from the table running. She went down the driveway, long-legged as a colt, piled into the car and then she was gone. And again for a moment the years unreeled in quick flashback to a time, so short a time in years, when she was a squirming bundle swathed in a blanket, a cry in the night.

The two littlest ones came later. They came in with their hair tousled and their faces not too well washed, the little boy had his pants buttoned crooked and the little girl hadn't been able to tie her bow in the back. She came backing over to me and I tied it for her.

Then two more cars tooted outside, with younguns hanging out the windows, tightly stuffed as a coop of chickens, and with a last blowing of noses and admonitions about keeping clean at recess, the last two scampered out and were gone, leaving two slightly eggy kisses in farewell.

I finished the paper and my coffee and went on upstairs, sat down at the typewriter and started to work. For a while there was the sound of the housework going on, the clatter of dishes being washed, the hum of the vacuum, the ringing of the phone, the coming of the bread man, the laundry man, and the men to pick up the garbage.

Then suddenly there was silence. Not a sound through all the house. I got up and wandered down to the living room, and Mama was sitting there reading, and I picked up a magazine and tried to read.

But I kept listening for a sound I did not hear— a sound that until this year had not been out of my house for a dozen years almost—the noise of children's voices, and the sound of their scampering feet.

"Well," I said, finally, "how do you like it?"

"Like what?" she asked, putting down her magazine.

"This blessed peace we have looked forward to all these years," I said. "This silence. This tranquillity. This time of which we've dreamed, when all the kids were at school and the house was quiet."

She saw what I was driving at, I guess. She smiled a little wryly.

"It's not as good as I thought it would be," she said. "It's only been a few weeks now, but I still can't quite get used to it. I find myself listening for them, playing or squabbling, or mashing the cat and making him yell."

"It's a good thing, I guess, that it comes this way," I said. "Slowly and by degrees. They'll be back soon, and this afternoon and tonight they'll all be here, raising a great rumpus, and everything will be the same again. But it's a preview," I said, "of a time not too far off when they'll be really gone, to make their own homes, and raise their own brood, and here we'll sit, Grandpa and Grandma, wishing they'd write or phone, or come and bring the chillun. . . ."

"Shut up," she said, suddenly.

"All right," I said. "All I was doing was trying to say that this peace and quiet and freedom that parents look forward to enjoying in their later years are always bought at the price of loneliness. . . ."

"You don't have to tell me that," she said. "I've known it from the first day the first one went to school."

"Clair de Lune" Put Brewster to Sleep

Every morning just about daylight a small red rooster which my children have named Brewster, but which I prefer to call Stonewall because of his resolute spirit, comes up from the woods back of my house and stands under my window and flaps his wings and cuts loose with a crow you can hear for a quarter of a mile.

This rouses a little feisty dog or maybe a fox terrier which lives down the street, and the small fat beagle which lives across the street, and they come tearing into my yard and take out after old Brewster, yipping and yowling and nipping at his tail feathers.

This arouses Mama, who leaps from her bed and rushes out into the yard in her nightgown carrying a broom or an umbrella or whatever she can lay hands on, and the neighbors are thus treated to the very curious sight of a small red rooster running madly about squawking and flapping, pursued by two small dogs who are yapping and barking, with a pretty grey-haired lady in her nightgown pursuing them and shouting at them and attempting to belabor them with a broom.

Sometimes, of course, Mama does not get there in time to

rescue Brewster, and the dogs catch him. They do not seem to want to hurt him much. They just munch on him a little, pulling out his tail feathers and breaking his wing feathers and bruising him until he gets into a state of shock. Then they go away and leave him alone, and he gets up and shakes himself and crows mightily in defiance, and they come back and the chase starts all over again.

I have been brooding over what to do about Brewster to repair the spiritual and physical trauma which he endures with such fortitude, so for the past two or three evenings when he has come quaaaarrrking around my chair while I am sitting out in the backyard listening to the blue jays cuss the crows down in the woods, I have been picking him up gently and taking him into the house to bed down on the top step of the basement stairs. After what he goes through all day, I figured he at least ought to have a good night's sleep.

Last night, though, after a rough day with the dogs, he seemed to be nervous and tense. When I put him in the basement and shut the door, I could hear him mumbling and muttering to himself nervously. So I picked him up and took him over to Ben Shute's house.

Every evening just at sunset, Ben, who paints pictures all day, plays beautiful music on the piano to relax his nerves, and I thought it might be soothing to old Brewster to hear Ben play. So Ben played for Brewster, Chopin and Debussy and other soft and soothing melodies and old Brewster sat there on the lid of the piano, his bright red comb nodding to the music of "Clair de Lune," until he got so sleepy he fell off the piano and I had to take him home.

The First Warm Winds of Spring

The first robin and the first jonquil arrived in my backyard simultaneously the other morning, as if blown there together on the first warm wind of spring. The jonquils were a little scrawny and puny looking, a little limp-necked, as if perhaps they hadn't slept well under the earth during the strange winter past. It may be that the changing weather, now warm, now cold, kept waking them up and they had trouble getting back to sleep.

The robin, on the other hand, was as fine and fat a robin as I ever saw. I don't know where he spent the winter, but wherever it was, he didn't miss any meals. He stood up straight with his head back and his chest out, and the sun shone on his russet breast like the shine on a polished apple.

I sometimes think the robins are my favorite birds. They don't ask any favors of man except that he leave just a little open ground not covered by asphalt. He never comes to the feeders, for there is nothing there that he wants. He is strictly a carnivore, in a miniscule way, living on the protein provided by worms and the little bugs that live in the grass. He has dignity also, and a certain sense of the fitness of things. Right now, as I look out the window, three doves are walking fast behind each other on the ground, and in the pine tree, a pair of doves sitting on a limb keep sidling toward each other. Those little sparrows with black eyebrows are all over the place, whirling and swirling in their springtime courtship. But the old robin just stands there in the middle of the lawn, surveying all this, as if saying, "Tut, tut, young people. Do not let yourselves be carried away."

The two first jonquils, as I mentioned, are pitiful little fellows, and one of them has had part of its fluted cap eaten away by a bug or a worm. But the old robin is now working over in the jonquil bed, which is bad news for the bug, or the worm. It will not long survive to eat another flower.

So nature works to keep life going and all things in balance in one small backyard, on the first fine day of almost-spring.

Shim Misses His Snoozing Place

If they don't bring the old green sofa back pretty soon, I'm afraid I'm going to have to take my dog Shim to a psychiatrist. He shows signs of losing his marbles. He was out in the backyard somehere fussing at squirrels, I suppose, when they came to get the sofa to take it away to have it fixed.

Then along about sundown he came and bumped at the door, as is his custom, and somebody let him in. He bowed and snuffled his thanks, paused a moment at the register to let the hot air waft over him—and send a faint perfume of shaggy dog over the house. Then he trotted in to jump up on the sofa to take his snooze, as has been his custom ever since he was a puppy with legs so short somebody had to boost him up.

I was sitting there watching as he came into the living room. He trotted right on over and crouched to make his spring, when suddenly he realized there was no sofa there. He was the most surprised little dog you ever saw. His eyebrows lifted till his eyes showed white. He sat down and stared, wrinkling his forehead as if in thought. He meditatively scratched a flea. Then he looked all around the room.

He trotted out into the hall and looked. It wasn't there. He trotted into the breakfast room and looked. No sofa. He came back and sat down and peered again at the empty space. Then he started making these strange little whimpering sounds deep in his throat, like a child about to cry.

Every evening now, since the sofa has been gone, he's gone through the same process.

To tell the truth, I'll be about as glad as he to see the old sofa come home. It was the first piece of furniture we ever bought. Long before we were married, Mama—though she wasn't a mama then, thank goodness—took five dollars out of my twenty-five-dollar salary every week and squirreled it away until she had enough to buy a sofa and an easy chair. It was Depression time then, and money was scarce and so were jobs. We went down to a furniture factory and had the old sofa made, the only job, I think, the factory had all week. It was sturdy and strong and it has lasted all these years while four children grew up spilling things on it and bouncing on it.

One corner of it always belonged to old Shim.

But I've got news for him. When the sofa comes back from the shop all rebuilt like new, with fancy new slipcovers, Mama's not going to let him sleep on it any more. And is *that* going to cause a battle! For he's a strong-willed dog, and she is a lady who knows her mind. But I bet I know who wins. For somehow home is not the same without old Shim over there in his accustomed place, sprawled out snoozing and snoring in peace and deep content.

Anybody Need a Squirrel?

If anybody is suffering from a shortage of squirrels around his house, let him see me. I am going into the squirrel-trapping business. I am weary of yelling "Shoo" at squirrels, and throwing rocks at them, and chasing them across the yard trying to switch them with a switch. I am now ready to take drastic measures, causing a huge shift in the squirrel population.

Until last Sunday, I had assumed, somehow, that a squirrel, being a suspicious and distrustful animal by nature, was too smart to be caught in a trap. I have found out differently. A squirrel is stupid. You can catch him in a trap over and over again if you want to. He does not seem to mind being caught in a trap.

But to go back to the beginning. Last Sunday I was sitting by the window peering out at the backyard and the scuppernong arbor, just beginning to put on its first faint feathery leaf, and the black, shiny trunks of the rain-washed trees. It was a peaceful scene but as usual there was a flaw in it. The flaw was that the birds, which should have been down at the bird feeder stuffing themselves, were up in the trees chirping hungrily, and the squirrels, who should have been up in the trees, were down at the bird feeder stuffing themselves on birdseed.

So I brooded over this situation for awhile, and I decided I would thwart the squirrels. Knowing that it is a squirrel's instinct to bury a nut, just as it is a dog's instinct to bury a bone, I put some peanuts on the bird feeder. And sure enough the squirrels came and grabbed the peanuts, and hustled off to the woods with them, which gave the birds time to swoop down and grab a few bites before the squirrels came back for another nut.

Then a small nuthatch threw a monkey wrench into the proceedings. He observed a peanut on the bird feeder, so he hopped up on the peanut, holding it is his claws, and began to peck a hole in the shell to get at the inside. And the squirrels came back and observed the nuthatch eating the peanut. So they stopped grabbing the peanuts and running off in the woods with them. They just sat there, shelling the peanuts, and eating them on the spot, jerking their tails and scaring the birds away when they tried to come back to feed.

This posed a problem. So I wandered around until I found a little flowerpot holder shaped like a birdcage and open at the bottom. I tied a long strip to this device and went upstairs and leaned out the window, poising the cage contraption over the bird feeder which hangs on the sill of the downstairs window. Then, when the squirrel sat up to eat the peanut, I dropped this cage, kerplunk, down over his head. But he was too quick for me. As soon as he felt the cage coming down around his ears, he shrugged it off with his forearms, like a man peeling off a slipover sweater, and was gone in a flash.

So I abandoned this idea, and searched around some more until I found a tin box about a foot long and about six inches wide. Then I put a little pile of peanuts out on one of the flagstones on the walk, and propped this box up with a little stick, and tied a string to the stick, and ran it across the yard, and through a crack in the door into the living room. Then I sat there holding the string, and sure enough there came a squirrel after the peanuts. And I jerked the string and the box fell and caught him.

I did not wish to hurt him, of course, but I did wish to scare him out of his wits. So I went out and beat on the top of the box with a stick, and scuffed it around on the flagstone, churning him around inside. Then I lifted the edge of the box about an inch, expecting to see him paralyzed with terror.

On the contrary, he had not even dropped his peanut. He was sitting there twirling it in his forepaws, gnawing the shell off, and he was glaring at me as if to say: "Shut the door, Buster, I feel a draft."

So I lifted up the box, and he grabbed one last peanut and took off. And while he was up in a tree eating his peanut, another one came along and I caught him, and then the first one came back, and I caught him again. All afternoon I caught squirrels and turned them loose. They seemed to think it was some sort of a game.

But I have not yet admitted defeat. I am going to get me a big wire cage, and fill it up with squirrels, and if nobody wants them, I am going to take them up to Pickens County, and turn them loose on the backside of Burnt Mountain, where they'll have to work for a living. That'll learn 'em!

Shim Comes Back Into the Family

All is well now between the world and my dog Shim. The great decision has been made. He can climb up on the sofa again. For ten years, I guess, the old sofa with the flower design slipcovers on it was his home.

Every night when the family gathered in the living room, he'd take his place over in the righthand corner, with his head resting on the low arm of the sofa. And there he'd sleep and doze and occasionally rouse to scratch a flea, and now and then he'd rise and stretch and jump down heavily and go back to see if somebody had put something in his bowl, and then he'd come back and jump up on the sofa again. Sometimes when it was raining he'd come in wet, with his paws all muddy, and jump up on the sofa and go to sleep. But nobody minded very much, for it was an old sofa that children had romped on for years and spilled things on and there wasn't much a little fat dog could do to hurt it.

Then about a year ago Mama decided that the old sofa was a shame and a disgrace and it had to go. But it was the first piece of furniture we ever owned, bought with our own money. And it was a good strong sofa, built to order back in

Depression times, when workmen built things honest and strong.

We didn't have the heart to sell it. So we just sent it down and had it rebuilt and when it came back it was the handsomest thing you ever saw, with all its busted springs repaired and the cushions repacked and all refinished in a fine brown cloth with threads of gold in it.

And of course a little muddy dog could not be allowed to sleep on such a magnificent sofa anymore. And I think that telling him that caused some sort of psychic trauma, for he began to grow listless and dispirited. Every night he'd come and look up beseechingly, going "eunh, eunh, eunh," whining to be allowed to jump up on the sofa. And every night we'd tell him, "NO," and his ears would droop and he'd go off and lie down in a corner and look sad.

Then last night, we were sitting there and he was over in the corner looking sad and Mama looked at him, and she looked just as sad. "Poor old fellow," she said. "His muzzle is getting white. He is begining to get stiff in his joints. He ought not to have to lie on that hard, cold floor. He ought to be comfortable in his old age. Let's take a vote."

"Aye," I said. "Whee!" Nancy said.

"Shim," Mama said. He looked up, dully. She patted the sofa beside her.

The years fell away. He stood up. His eyes grew bright. Like a fuzzy brown cannonball he lunged across the room and Whoomp, he landed on the sofa. He was so beside himself he turned around six times instead of three, to make a nest. Then he lay down and heaved a great sigh of happiness and went to sleep.

He was back in the family again, and everybody was glad.

Brewster Finds His Harem in the Hills

My rooster, Brewster, may not last long, but at the moment, from all I hear, he is living in a kind of rooster heaven, complete with harem. What happened was this. The longer we kept Brewster around the house here in town, the more noticeable became the chill between us and our neighbors.

They would inquire sweetly about Brewster's health, pointing out that when he woke them up with his crowing at five o'clock that morning he sounded as if he had a touch of laryngitis. They hoped that Brewster wasn't suffering from bronchitis or the croup or anything that might cause his untimely demise.

Now they are nice neighbors, and we did not wish a rooster to come between us and them, so at a sorrowful family council it was decided that Brewster had to go.

So one of the youngsters who was driving up to the mountain took Brewster up there and dropped him off at Oley Cantrell's house, Oley being the caretaker at the mountain who gives a home to all sorts of pets, such as cats and puppies, which city folks find they cannot keep.

Oley had already gone to bed when Brewster arrived and

my son John, who was delivering Brewster, did not see any sense in waking him up. So he just left Brewster on Oley's porch.

Now Oley takes up the story.

"About four-thirty in the morning I woke up with what sounded like the biggest rooster in the world crowing right under my window. I knew I did not have no rooster and I figured I must be dreaming I heard a rooster crow. But he crowed again, so loud it shuk the bed, and I looked out the window and there stood this little old half-banty red rooster, rared back, crowin'.

"He crowed so loud he woke up my hens who were roostin' in the backyard and they began to make a fuss. That was the first time, I reckon, he knew there was any hens in ten miles. So he took out after my hens, even if it was before sunup, and run them all over the mountain. He run them all day and till nearly about night. They didn't have a chance to lay an egg all day. They were scared to stop that long. That is the busiest rooster I ever saw."

Oley wasn't mad at Brewster for chasing his hens, but Oley's wife, Mary, was of a different mind. That rooster, she said, had to go. So Oley caught Brewster and took him down to Bill Bryan's house. But there weren't any hens at Bill's house. There were some pigeons and some ring-necked doves, but every time Brewster cocked his eye and started dragging his wing and shuffling, they took flight. So Brewster walked a mile and a half down the road and around the lake and up the hill to Oley's house.

He's there still, happy as any rooster you ever saw, with his harem clucking around him. But how long Oley's going to let him stay, I don't know. It may be we'll have to bring him home again to his lonely bachelor life on Normandy Drive.

But he's not going to like it a bit.

Chester and the Cat Show

Great excitement prevails among the younger element at my house. My cat, Chester, Jr., has been invited to enter the Cotton States Cat Show, to be held at the City Auditorium on the 27th and 28th of November, and they have already started getting Chester ready for his first public appearance, much to his vast disgust.

As soon as the announcement arrived that he had been accorded this singular honor, they snatched the poor old fellow off the sofa, soused him in a tub of water and started giving him a bath. Since Chester has had no water on his person since the last time he jumped into the sink by mistake, fleeing from a visiting pooch, this enraged him no end and he submitted to it only under the shrillest protest. Even when they dried him off his troubles were not over, for they insisted on touching up his whiskers with moustache wax, and they started to paint his toenails with red nail polish, but I put a stop to that.

They also wanted to put a little touch of perfume behind Chester's ear, but Chester himself put a stop to that. He swung a couple of left hooks that drew blood, wiggled out of their clutches and headed for the back door. Wax on the moustache, he seemed to say, was all right; but there were some things to which no self-respecting tomcat would submit.

I am a little worried about a few things in connection with Chester's entry into this cat show, anyway. There are going to be a lot of cats down there, gentleman cats and lady cats, and I shudder to think what might happen. All of those other cats are going to be very aristocratic and blue-blooded cats—Persians and Manxes and Abyssinians and Siamese and I don't know what all, and old Chester, who is just cat, may suffer from an inferiority complex in the presence of so much aristocratic feline blood.

On the other hand, he may decide that his reason for being there is solely to take a poke at any cat of the male persuasion which he sees, and I sadly fear that I may have to pay off heavily if Chester claws a twenty-five dollar chunk out of some high-toned cat who never was in a back-alley rough-and-tumble in his life. I also shudder to think what some lady cat-lover would do if she should see old Chester, a rowdy and a nobody, approaching one of her itsy bitsy tweetumses with an amorous gleam in his eye. She would probably have me and Chester both tossed out of the show on our ears.

I also trust that Mrs. W. E. Limpert, of Mentor, Ohio, and Mrs. C. F. Rotter, of Minneapolis, Minnesota, who are going to judge this cat show, carry ample insurance. I don't know how old Chester is going to behave when they take him out and stand him up on the table and start talking about the color of his eyes, the length of his whiskers, the angle at which he carries his tail, and whatever other points they consider in judging cats. He may behave all right. On the other hand, he may want no part of such foolishness, and claw the epidermis off of everybody in sight. Chester is not a high-strung cat. He just does not like anybody interfering with his rest.

Maybe it will turn out all right, though, and I am looking

forward to going down there and watching Chester strut around with all those fancy cats. I am very fond of cat shows, for cat people are very interesting people. They can purr as silkily when they are pleased—and claw as murderously when they aren't—as the ones on the inside. Maybe old Chester and I both had better be on our guard.

He Never Lost a Fight

Every time I look at my dog Shim I think of a line of verse I read somewhere long ago—"They went forth to battle, but they always fell." Old Shim is like that—old and stiff in the joints as he is, he is still the defender, guarding his house and his people against any dog that makes the mistake of straying on his home soil; and here lately, he always gets whipped.

People don't bother him. He likes people too much. In fact, I think if a burglar came by night and broke into the house and started making off with the family silver, old Shim would go out and watch him, placidly wagging the tuft of hair that serves him as a tail and feeling like he was being a big help.

But dogs are different. No matter how big they are, he'll have at them, scooting low along the ground and coming up at them from beneath. It's like being hit by a torpedo and many a dog is so taken aback he does not try to fight back. He just turns and hightails it for the street, with old Shim snapping at his haunches like an angry alligator.

Dogs are curious beasts, though, and as soon as they get to the street they turn on old Shim. They know he may own the lawn and the turnaround and the woods back of the house. But they know the public street belongs to them as much as it does to him. So the first thing I know they have got him down in the street and are about to eat him up.

He has never lost a yard fight and has never won a street fight. Which is why the veterinarian is so fond of old Shim. We are always taking him there with an ear half chewed off, or a big chunk bitten out of his flank, or a slash along his shoulder blade you could lay your finger in. The vet just sews him up and gives him a shot of penicillin and sends him on home.

In fact, I think when the weather gets warm I'll shave old Shim and count the sewed-up scars that mark his hide, just so I'll have some idea of how much his valiant defense of my household has cost me over the years. I may get to take it off my income tax, on the basis it's a misfortune wrought by nature, like a big tree being blown down, or an ice storm killing the shrubbery. For if a dog fight isn't a manifestation of nature in its more violent form, I don't know what is.

Swaggering Mouse Stole the Kleenex

Another good friend of mine up here in the mountains is a small brownish-colored mouse who comes every night to steal Kleenex. He is a very valiant mouse, having no fear of either man or beast. The box of Kleenex sits right by my bed and to get a piece of tissue out of the box he must come so close that I could easily reach out and slap him silly with a shoe.

To get to the box of Kleenex he has to pass right by the basket where my dog Shim takes his rest at night. This does not disturb him in the slightest.

On the other hand, it disturbs Shim. In fact, the way I know that the mouse is abroad and is on his way to steal my Kleenex is when I hear Shim begin to make little whimpering noises in his throat. Shim is a very brave dog when it comes to fighting other dogs. But he is dreadfullly afraid of mice, cats, cockroaches, and bees.

So when the mouse pauses at Shim's basket and pushes his nose through the wicker and tangles whiskers with Shim, Shim does not lift a paw to defend himself. He leaps from his basket, kerwhump, and I hear his paws go click, click across the floor and he goes and climbs up on the sofa.

For when the mouse is on the prowl old Shim heads for higher ground.

The mouse, of course, feels no ill will toward Shim. On his way home with the stolen Kleenex, he trots through Shim's basket and leaves his calling card.

Mama, of course, does not share my fondness for the little fellow and is always urging the cat to stay awake at night and ambush him. The cat, of course, does not care to stay around the house all night, having better things to do, and so far the mouse has gone his way unmolested. Until the other afternoon, that is.

Nobody is home except Mama and the cat, and they both are snoozing, when the mouse decides he is running short of Kleenex again. He comes swaggering across the floor and is tugging at a Kleenex when the cat rouses and spies him.

The cat leaps, knocking over the chair he is sleeping in, and the mouse runs.

Mama rouses in time to see the mouse run behind the chest of drawers in the corner. So she moves the chest of drawers and there in the corner is a ball of Kleenex, all chewed into tiny pieces, as big as a basketball.

And while Mama and the cat peer at this ball of Kleenex, it begins to wiggle and the mouse leaps and Mama leaps, all at once. And from then on for about ten minutes chaos seems to reign.

I get there just at the end of it. Kleenex is floating in the air like goose feathers, pictures are crooked on the wall, tables are overturned, and lamps are busted. The cat was staggering from a blow on the head by the broom with which Mama was attempting to annihilate the mouse. And the mouse was safe somewhere in the machinery of the refrigerator. Where he still is, so far as I know.

Chester Had to Have His Rest

I must apologize to the members of the fancy, which is what the cat people call themselves, for the conduct and appearance of my cat, Chester, Jr., when I took him down to participate in the cat show at the auditorium last weekend. Everybody at my house is naturally greatly excited about Chester, Jr., being in the cat show, and they are anxious for him to acquit himself well. So the afternoon before the show is to start, the younguns seize Chester, Jr., who is comfortably asleep on the sofa, and take him back and run a big tub full of warm water and give him a good scrubbing and then they dry him off and brush his fur with a brush, and part his whiskers neatly on each side and tie a ribbon around his neck, and touch him lightly behind the ear with some Chanel No. 5 and get him all ready.

So what does Chester, Jr., do that night? He does exactly the same thing he does every night. He sneaks out the back door along about moonrise and goes meowing off into the night seeking adventure. Evidently he finds more of it than he can cope with in one evening. The next morning when I open the back door he comes staggering in in the worst shape I have ever seen him. He has a gash over one eye about half an inch long, and he is walking on three legs because the other leg has been so badly chewed it does not function; and his nice pink ribbon is in tatters and is tied in a hard knot up under one ear, like a drunk man's necktie. He is soaking wet and muddy, and all in all he is the saddest-looking cat you ever saw in your life.

And here it is eight-thirty in the morning and Chester, Jr., has to be in his cage at the cat show at ten o'clock, looking respectable. So we seize Chester, Jr., and take him back and souse him in the tub again, and this time he does not take kindly to this process at all, for he is sore in every bone and all he wants is to find a warm place where he can lie down and lick his wounds and sleep and meditate on his sins. But we finally get him washed again, and dried off to some extent, so we wrap him up in a bath towel and rush him down to the auditorium, where they have a cage waiting for him.

There is a big smoke-colored tomcat on one side and a very seductive-looking lady cat, a Siamese, on the other. So what happens? The big tomcat reaches through the bars of his cage and gives Chester, Jr., a poke in the snoot, and Chester, Jr., does not even lift a paw in self-defense. And the lady cat on the other side meows at Chester, Jr., in an alluring manner and rubs up against the bars of the cage and Chester, Jr., ignores her also. He just curls up in one corner of his cage and puts his paws over his face to keep the light out of his eyes and goes to sleep.

I cannot stay to observe how Chester, Jr., conducts himself the rest of the day, but the ladies who are running the cat show say that Chester, Jr., does not stir from this position throughout the day. He just gets his rest, ignoring all that goes on in this vicinity. Later, some of the men who are attending the cat show tell me in confidence that they think Chester, Jr., is suffering from a hangover, as well as from bruises and contusions, but I think this is a slanderous statement.

Anyway, I am told that a good many nice people come by to speak to Chester, Jr., and to buy him little presents, such as rubber mice, and little balls of yarn with catnip in them which are supposed to amuse him, but he ignores all these things and continues to get his rest.

Even when they come to get him and take him up to the bench for judging, he just opens one eye, yawns drowsily, and goes to sleep while the judge is looking him over.

So it is no wonder that Chester, Jr., does no better than to win third prize in a field of four in the house cat class. But the people are very nice to Chester, Jr., and award him a sort of consolation prize. It is a kind of cat-show Oscar, carved of many beautiful woods, such as walnut, mahogany, mulberry, and maple, with a plastic cat with diamond eyes on the base of it. It is the work of L. P. McGee, who amuses himself by carving beautiful things in wood while his wife is busy with her cats, and it was a far nicer award than Chester, Jr., deserved, considering his scandalous behavior.

That Sad and Happy Last Day

For me, today is that sad and happy day that parents look forward to for years with mingled joy and dread. Tonight she'll be on a train, headed north to school, and the blowing of the train whistle deep in the night may make her feel a little lonely and homesick for her tumbled room at home, and for the kid sister and brothers she has loved and fought with all these years.

And I know how it's going to be with me. I'll wake up around midnight, about the time she usually comes in from a date, listening for the sound of her voice in the quiet dark, whispering, "Hey, I'm home." And for this first Sunday night in a long, long time, ever since she started going out on dates, three, maybe four years ago, I wait to hear it. And I'm going to feel a little lonesome, too. For whether she knows it or not, you never really come home again, once you've gone off to school, for a door has closed that can never be opened again, and all life, in the future, is an opening of new doors, each of which leads farther away from home.

In a way, though, I'm glad the day has come at last. A mama getting her daughter ready to go off to school is about as frenzied a creature as a mama getting her daughter ready to be wed, and in neither situation is a father of much use around the house.

He can't read in the living room, for they're in there trying on new clothes, and he can't go back to his own lair to find refuge, for the sewing woman's there. And everywhere he turns, he stumbles over boxes and trunks and suitcases, and he's up to his knees in string and tissue paper, and everywhere his eye falls there's a charge account slip, showing where they've bought something that costs $26.82 plus tax.

All of this, of course, is necessary to getting an education, and I don't object to it, for I'm getting a little education, too. I've found out that if you put some dark blue ink on the frayed cuff of an old blue suit, the white lining hardly shows through at all. I'm still making a study of what to do about the shine on the seat of the pants, and before she's finished her four-year course, I bet you I'll have solved that problem, too.

Right at the last, of course, something always goes wrong, and this time it was really tragic. Her trunk went on ahead, with all the pretty dresses in it, and the little hats with wispy veils on them, and the shoes and bags that match, and all the stuff a lady has to have to really dress up. And it wasn't until it was gone that she thought about her date.

That last date before you go off to school is a very important one, for you have to look dreamier than you ever looked in your life, so you'll leave him so stunned and shaken he won't forget you during all the months you'll be gone. And she'd forgotten that and packed every blessed thing she owned except some scuffed old loafers and some beat-up shorts and sweaters.

It's a good thing that girls grow tall these days and can wear their mamas' clothes. And it's a good thing, too, that mamas keep themselves slim and dress in clothes much like their daughters wear.

She might have looked just a wee bit on the matronly side, going out on that last date, but a touch of perfume back of the ear fixed that, all right. And I'll bet he was just as dazzled as she hoped he would be. And I'll bet he will miss her like the dickens when she's gone. I know I will.

Broadus the Cat Buffaloes Dogs

I have been making a study of my new cat Broadus, and I have come to the conclusion that he has faith. I don't know who or what he has faith in, but whatever it is, it sustains him nobly. He is, for example, the only cat I ever saw who does not stand in a doorway, hesitating, while he surveys the backyard to see if there is a dog out there. He doesn't care whether there is a dog out there or not. He just stalks out without reconnoitering.

Sometimes there *is* a dog out there. In fact, if it is early in the morning, there may be three or four dogs, for there is a dawn patrol of dogs that comes through my backyard every morning. There is an old underslung basset hound who always looks as if he is about to cry—maybe because his ears are so long he steps on them—and a big brown boxer that looks as if he has been hit on the nose with a baseball bat, and a big white boxer, and a lady beagle named Daisy.

They always come by my house every morning to investigate my dog Shim to see if there has been any change in the situation since last they met.

Sometimes my cat Broadus stalks out just as these dogs

are passing by, and I think to myself, "Uh-oh, this is going to be rough on old Broadus."

But old Broadus does not think so. Looking as if there is not a dog in the world, he stalks out to the middle of the turnaround and sits down to wash his face. The dogs stop trotting from bush to bush, making their investigations, and they sit down and stare at Broadus. Then they look at each other, and you can see they are thinking.

"Here is this cat," they are thinking, "and we do not like cats, and we have got him outnumbered four to one, and if somebody got him by the hind leg and somebody else got him by the front leg and somebody else got him in the middle—then we'd have him."

So they sit there, cogitating, with their foreheads all wrinkled up, for about five minutes. And Broadus sits there washing his face, and you can see the big muscles in his forelegs swell under the soft fur. And he finishes washing and lifts his tail straight up in the air stiff as a broom handle and walks toward those dogs, and they give way before him like the Red Sea parting for the Children of Israel, and he stalks past them as if they weren't there, and goes on off down into the woods.

And they look at each other with a kind of foolish look on their faces, and all at once they trot off down the street.

The Green Dean Comes to Live

The voice on the phone was a little girl's voice. She said she was so glad I was going to give their parrot a good home and her papa and mama would be right over with it. Then she hung up. "Who was that?" Mama said, looking up from her reading. "Beats me," I said. "Somebody must have got a wrong number. It was a little girl. Said she was bringing me a parrot."

"Oh my goodness!" Mama said. "Don't you remember? You were sitting there signing books and looking confused and the bishop came up to you and said that Dean and Ann Hardman up at the Cathedral had a parrot they couldn't keep and would you like to have it and you said sure."

"Me?" I said, "incredible."

"You," she said.

Then the doorbell rang and there stood the Dean, in his turnabout collar, and Ann, and Mary Lee, the little girl who had called me. And they were staggering under the weight of a parrot cage that stood about as high as the Tower of Pisa.

And now my living room looks like an aviary, or apiary, or whatever the name is. One is a place you keep birds, and the other a place you keep bees, though you'd think it was a place to keep apes.

Anyway, I am now the proud owner of a small, belligerent-looking parrot, who is named the Green Dean because of his color and his ecclesiastical background.

And I see already that he and I are going to have trouble. For, as befits a clergyman's parrot, he has been living in a cage that is almost monkish in its austerity, with nothing but a bar to sit on and a little cup for his water and his sunflower seed.

But I have already discovered that there is nothing monkish about this parrot. He is a real high liver at heart—a Sybarite. For, as soon as he sees my parakeet Bismarck's cage, with its fancy trappings, including swings and mirrors and little jingling bells and a music box that plays a happy tune, he flutters over there and swaggers in and starts looking at himself in Bismarck's mirror and preening himself and going "Aaark," and then he starts swinging on Bismarck's swings and butting Bismarck's bells to make them swing and tinkle and playing Bismarck's music box by sitting on the little perch that makes it play.

And poor old Bismarck does not know what to make of this burly stranger who has arrived so suddenly. And now, after all these years of tranquillity in my house, it looks as if I'm going to have to be an umpire between a parrot and a parakeet.

School Days Start the Morning Storms

Was it only yesterday that the world was quiet? It's hard to remember now, for it seems so long ago. A man could wake up and go in and put coffee on, and stand there yawning, waiting for the water to boil, and the bubble of the boiling water was the only sound in the house.

Brown and soaked by the sun, the kids slept on while the day brightened. Snoozed on and on while the good smell of the making coffee drifted through the house. Even the dog stayed asleep. A man could pour his coffee then and go sit on the porch with never a stirring in the house to trouble him, never a peep or a sound.

Now that peace is gone. In the cold gray dawn, bells start ringing all over the house, and always there's a loud thump or two upstairs where a groping hand, reaching to shut off the alarm, knocks the clock to the floor. Then the plumbing starts to roar in the walls, and the sound of violent altercations rises on the air—"Are you going to stay in there all morning?" "Aw, shuddup!"

Then the voices start bellowing down the stair. "Ma-meee—I don't see any socks, Ma—mee—I can't find a handkerchief." Mommy this, Mommy that, and Mama's in the kitchen, cutting cantaloupe with one hand and frying bacon with the other, and scrambling eggs with the other, and making toast with the other. Which makes her an octopus. At least a lady *should* be an octopus to get three kids off to school in the morning.

Then down they come, feet thundering on the stair, and the foul ritual of breakfast takes place—a most revolting sight. One gulps his orange juice too fast, and it spills out on his clean, fresh shirt; and he has to be sent back upstairs to change shirts. And another, trying to read a comic book while she eats, misses her mouth with a fork full of eggs and spills scrambled eggs in her lap, and she has to be sent back to change.

Then the yelling for money begins. I don't know why we delude ourselves by saying we have a system of "free" schools. What's free about it I don't know. It's two bits for this and a half a dollar for that and two bucks for something else—and "Mommy, Coach said if I didn't get that busted cleat fixed on my football shoe he wasn't going to let me practice because I'd hurt somebody."

"Ma—meee's" financial resources don't last very long, which means that Pop's pants pockets come in for a thorough searching.

Finally, when the last one has been sent back upstairs to brush teeth, or wet hair and stick it down, or to scrub hands, there comes a squeal of tires on the driveway, and an impatient tooting. And the mama who is driving that day is sitting there, looking harassed and a little wild-eyed, with the back seat full of young, all engaged in violent altercation. So you shoo your own out, half-scrubbed, half-brushed, still with egg on them, and off they go to the first day at school.

Then a blessed peace and quiet falls on the house at last. It lasts about three minutes. Then the bread man comes, and the garbage man, banging the cans, and the man who wants to know, "Y'all want any yard work done?" and the phone starts ringing, and the day is in its stride.

It is a terrible thing to contemplate that this same uproar will break out, every morning except Saturday and Sunday, from now until June. And I have come to the conclusion that a father has no place in it. The best thing for him to do is to get up when the first alarm goes off upstairs, and toss his pants, with the pockets full of quarters and half dollars, out in the hall where they can be looted easily.

Then he should get back in bed and stick his head under the pillow and try to ride out the storm as best he can, until they are gone.

Old Galahad Adjusts to His New Home

I can tell already that my new tomcat, Galahad, is going to be a big help around the house. He's got to get a few things straight in his mind, of course, such as who owns the place, meaning me, and who doesn't own it, meaning him. And he might as well understand right now that I'm not going to sleep in that box in the kitchen, the one with the old towel folded up in it.

He is. Either there or on the floor.

And he's not going to sleep in that bed back in the bedroom, the one with the electric blanket on it. I am. We got all that settled last night. Or I guess we did.

Anyway we reached a sort of compromise. He didn't sleep under the blanket with his head on the pillows as he insisted on doing. He slept at the foot on top of the covers. Every time I wiggled a foot under the blanket he sank his claws into it. Also his teeth.

I guess he thought there was a chipmunk hiding there. He's got to knock that off, otherwise he's going to be right back down there where he came from—in a cage at the Humane Society squalling his head off for somebody to adopt him again.

HAROLD MARTIN REMEMBERS

We get along all right in the daytime, though. When I come home and find him in my chair he moves over two or three inches, just as polite as you please. He doesn't mind my sitting in my chair at all, so long as I don't lean back and mash him. When that happens he scratches. The doctors say it is good for a man to sit upright on the edge of his chair. It develops proper posture.

I don't know what kind of mouser he is. We are a little short of mice lately, due to one of these exterminating companies that comes around once a month and kills one mouse and three roaches and charges you five dollars.

He's a fine squirreler, though. Every morning when I get up he is sitting at the window glaring at the squirrels eating at the bird feeder. His eyes are popped out with eagerness and his tail is twitching like a tiger's.

I pick him up gently and, carrying him at the hip like a sawed-off shotgun, I slip out the back door and around the side of a big bush that grows by the bird feeder. I aim him at the squirrel and turn him loose and he sails through the air like a catapult. He lands on the bird feeder and the squirrel takes off and he takes off after the squirrel in a great shower of flying birdseed, and then there is the greatest chase you ever saw, across the terrace and the yard until the squirrel leaps to the oak tree and whisks up it to the first fork, where he sits for an hour, jerking his tail angrily and cussing Galahad.

Which suits me fine, for while the squirrel is up in the tree cussing Galahad and Galahad is under the tree glaring at the squirrel, the birds swarm to the feeder and stuff themselves. And now if I can just figure out how to teach him it's okay to chase squirrels but chasing birds is against the law, everything's going to be all right.

He Was Always Losing Something

"You know my pot?" he said.

"Your what?" I said, looking up from my paper.

"Pot," he said. "Stummick, that big stummick you used to be all a time kidding me about."

"What about it?" I said.

"It's gone," he said. "I've lost it."

"You are always losing things," I said. "Where do you suppose you left it?"

"I know where I left it," he said. "Over at Northside, on the football field. I just knew today it was gone. I was sitting there on the bench and you know how it used to stick out (he made a gesture with his hands like a man carrying a watermelon in front of him). Well, I looked down and it wasn't there. It was flat."

"That's fine," I said. "Maybe I ought to come over there and get flattened out a little. How do you go about it?"

"You better not," he said. "You'd fall on your face. You wheeze when you just walk up the driveway."

"Never mind," I said. "When I was your age I was all muscle. I was like a rock."

"Yeah," he said. "Stone Mountain."

"Quiet," I said. "But tell me more about this miracle. How is it that you have changed from a roly-poly little fat boy—a blubber tub, so to speak—all of a sudden?"

"Coach did it," he said. "He banks us. You know that steep bank. He makes all the fat boys run up and down it. 'Okay, all you fatsos,' he says. 'Up that bank twenty-five times.' So we run up it. And pretty soon our stummicks are gone. It makes you feel good when your stummick is gone. I got hit right in the stummick with a football. It didn't even hurt. People butt me in the stummick with their helmets on. They just bounce off."

"Supper's on," Eva yelled from the kitchen. He rose as if on springs. I watched him go out the door. It was like watching a stranger. Two weeks ago he was a chunky little round guy, bouncing on the springboard up at the mountain. Now the muscles were rippling under his tight shirt. He was spreading out at the shoulders. He stood taller in the doorway than I remembered him. Maybe it was my imagination, but his voice had sounded deeper.

Seems like it was only yesterday I was peering through a glass window at Piedmont Hospital, watching him kick and gurgle in his basket. Now he was growing up. The baby bloom was melting off him. The contours of a man, the lean hard muscles were coming through.

Part of it was football, of course, and the hard charging up and down that steep bank in the hot sun. But most of it was the roll of the wheel of time—the wonderful process of growing up, of passing suddenly from chubby little boyhood into the wonderland of strong-muscled youth.

It's a proud thing for a man to watch his son grow up. Even though it does make him feel all of a sudden fat and soft, and creaky-jointed and old.

A Parrot Wants His Coffee

If anybody wants to know how to get revenge on a parrot, I think I have found a way. My parrot, the Green Dean, has been harassing me out of my wits every morning. I get up in the cold gray dawn and go out and fix the coffee and the Green Dean does not stir beneath the covers of his cage except to utter a sleepy "Qrrk" or two. Then about the time the kettle begins to whistle, he begins to move about.

He tries to whistle like the kettle but there is no melody in it. It sounds more like a policeman on a busy corner whistling angrily at a jaywalker.

Then when I get my cup of coffee and sit down in my chair and start to read the paper, he sets up a clamor to be let out. He sounds like a maniac, shrieking and shouting, for he smells the coffee and he wants some. But he won't let me give him any coffee. He looks at me with an angry eye as if he thinks I am trying to poison him. Then he lets out a wild shriek for Mama.

So she comes out, sleepy, in her robe, and fixes a cup of coffee and goes over to the cage and he hops out on her shoulder, shouting at the top of his voice until she gives him his coffee, spoonful by spoonful. Then he wants a cigarette, like the rest of us. He doesn't want to smoke it. He wants to tear it up.

After he's had his coffee and his cigarette, he flies over and lands on the top of Bismarck the parakeet's cage, and he squawks at poor old Bismarck until he crouches in terror in the corner of his cage.

He spends the rest of the day arguing with the television, and fussing at Miss Eva every time she comes through the room. He keeps up a machine gun fire of awks, arrks, whistles, and urrhs all day, saying nothing that makes sense, but yapping all the time.

We fixed him the other afternoon, though. Some friends of my daughter came by, squealing their joyful congratulations on her engagement, and you know how it is when females get together to talk about somebody's getting engaged. It is noisier than a whole tree full of parrots.

The poor old Green Dean knew he had finally met his match. He crawled mutely into his cage, not even uttering a chirp in all the clamor. And he's hardly had a word to say since.

Courting in the Mountain Rain

Along about midnight the moon went out and it began to rain again, slow and drizzly, and a gray fog drifted wetly in the windows of the little place in the mountains.

"Maybe you'd better go get him," his mama said from her bed. "I hate to think of his walking home in the dark. He's wearing his white saddle oxfords. They'll get all muddy."

"I hate to think of riding that road in the dark," I said. "I'd be wearing my white sidewall tires. They'll get all muddy. If he's old enough to go courting, he's old enough to get home by himself."

"He's just a little boy," his mama said.

"He's sixteen going on seventeen," I said. "He stands five feet twelve inches high. He weighs 205 pounds, and he's got muscles made out of the same stuff they make golf ball covers out of."

"He'll get soaked," his mama said, "and he hasn't got a flashlight."

"He's wearing his ten-gallon cowboy hat," I said. "That's like being under a tent. And he stays soaked all day. He goes into the lake in the morning and he doesn't come out until dark."

"You go get him," his mama said.

"I'm asleep," I said.

"It's dark on that road," she said. "There may be snakes."

"The snakes," I said, "are all in bed, like me. And as long as this rain lasts they'll stay there. Like me."

"He still can't see the road," she said, "not without a flashlight."

"He'll borrow a light," I said, "or maybe the love light in his eyes will light the way."

"Phooey," she said, and I heard her stirring about, groping for her slippers.

"Awright, awright," I said, "I'll go."

I looked out the window, down the road. Dimly in the mist a yellow light was glowing. Behind it a strange shape loomed. It seemed to have antlers on its head. He came in. He was wet and mad. He was carrying an old-fashioned kerosene lamp in one hand. There was no chimney on it. In the other he carried his white saddle oxfords. What was left of them. He threw his shoes on the floor. And his hat. He was growling like a bear.

"Nice walk?" I said.

"Lookita shoes," he said. "Lookita hat."

"What happened?" I said.

"I left 'em on the front porch at her house," he said. "They were wet. The dog ate 'em."

That explained the antlered look. The crown of his cowboy hat was chewed into tatters. The top of one shoe was gnawed off. The heel of the other was gone.

"You walk all the way?" I asked.

"Twice," he said. "I got nearly home. Things were walking about in the woods, sounded like. Maybe it was just the rain dripping off the bushes. I couldn't walk fast, for the lamp would go nearly out. I saw this thing by the road. It moved. I said, 'Who's that?' It was Katherine from down at the Bryans'. She was going up to sleep in the Winship's servants' house. She got lost. She was just wandering around in the dark. I took her back to the Winship's house. Then I came on home."

"What happened to the lamp chimney?" I said.

"It got broke," he said. "When I saw this thing move, I jumped. It just sailed through the air and broke." He put on his cowboy hat. His short-cropped head poked through the top. The jagged edges stuck up like deer horns. He went on to bed.

"Did you see that hat?" I said, trying to choke back the laughter.

"It's your fault," his mama said. "You should have gone for him."

"Did I chew up his hat?" I said. "Did I gnaw on his shoes?"

"Oh, go to sleep," his mama said.

Parrots Talk a Lot, But Say Little

That parrot, the Green Dean, has gone back to his former owners with our embarrassed apologies, and it is clear now that I am going to miss him—about like I would miss an aching tooth that has suddenly quit hurting.

The trouble with the Green Dean was the same thing that is the trouble with a lot of us. He talked all the time, but nothing he ever said made much sense.

As soon as I walked out into the living room in the morning, headed for the kitchen to make coffee, he'd set up this querulous squawking under the covers of his cage. I'd make the coffee and come back in and offer him a spoonful, and from the racket he raised you'd think I'd tried to wring his neck. He didn't want me to give him his coffee. He wanted Mama to give it to him. And he wanted to sit on her shoulder while he drank it.

So Mama, who is a patient soul and loves all sorts of little furred and feathered creatures, would stumble out sleepy-eyed and fix the Dean his coffee. Then he'd set up another wild and angry harangue. It turned out he didn't want his coffee until he'd had his orange juice.

So she'd give him his orange juice, holding the glass

almost on its side, and he'd stick his head down in the glass and utter a weird shriek. And I don't know why it is but a parrot shrieking with his head in a glass sets up sound waves that pierce the human eardrums like ice picks, and causes sleeping dogs to rise and howl.

After he'd had his orange juice, he'd start in on his coffee. He'd take a sip of coffee and then pinch Mama on the ear with his sharp beak. He'd take another sip and grab an eyebrow and tug until he'd pulled it out. Ladies pull their own eyebrows without obvious pain, but it is different, I gather, when a parrot pulls a lady's eyebrow out. Anyway, Mama would utter a cry of pain and swipe at him and with a great flurry of wings he would fly up onto the lampshade, blowing all the ashes out of the ashtray into my coffee cup.

Then he would sit on the lampshade and fuss at me, and Mama, and the dog, and my poor old parakeet, Bismarck, until Miss Eva came to work. Then he'd spend the day fussing at Miss Eva, and tearing newspapers into bits and throwing them on the floor.

This, of course, did not please Miss E. and I caught her one day about to wreak a terrible revenge on the parrot. She had taken the nozzle off the vacuum cleaner hose and was advancing on the Dean. She was planning on sucking him into the vacuum cleaner.

Naturally, I chided her for this and she played her trump. "Either that bird goes, or I go," she said.

So the Dean went. He's back in the study of the long-suffering clergyman who gave him to me.

It Was a Long Journey,
In More Ways Than One

The phone rang at the office, and Mama said there was a man there at the house who said he used to know me and would like to say "hello." So I said hello, puzzled and wondering, and all he said was "Hi," but that was enough.

He was home again after three months and 12,000 miles of roving and rambling, working where he could find work, and moving on when the job ended.

And sometimes he had slept in a bed and eaten thick steaks at restaurants, and sometimes he had slept on the ground and eaten out of cans.

So I went home early and as soon as I saw him I knew he'd changed. He wasn't a kid anymore. The hand he stuck out to me was as hard and rough as a piece of wood, calloused and strong from hard work.

And when I put my hand on his shoulder it was like laying it on a piece of carved furniture, the hard, smooth muscles thick and tough from wrestling with the wheel of a big truck carrying heavy loads on winding mountain roads. And he was lean and slim and tough and the baby bloom, the softness, was all gone out of him.

The big change was not physical. It was inside, in his

heart and mind. He had seen a side of life he had never known before.

He had lived with the migrant workers, the Indians, the Mexicans, the drifters from Oklahoma who follow the crops year in and year out, who have never known, and never will know, a better home than a picker's shack beside a pea-field, a bunkhouse where the hands sleep during the wheat harvest.

He had learned what he had never suspected—how hard it is for a man who works with his muscles to make a dollar, and how much sweat and pain it takes to make just enough to buy something to eat, and a saggy bed in a shabby motel, and enough gas to move on when the job is done.

He had learned how slow the dollars come in, and how fast they go out. And somewhere along the line he learned that it is important for a man to stand on his own two feet and pay his own way. So the first thing he did when he got home was to pull out a roll of rumpled bills and pay his mama back the $200 she had given him when he started on his trip.

He liked every minute of it, he said—Tennessee, Kentucky, Indiana, Illinois, Minnesota, Montana, the Dakotas, Idaho, Washington, Oregon, the great panorama of the California coast, and the lonely sweep of desert on the long ride home.

Even when there was nothing to see, it was exciting, for wherever it was, it was new to his eyes, and far from home. And he'd learned that among the poor, the sweating, the illiterate and uncouth migrant workers there was a great deal of kindness, and gentleness, and humor.

The man who taught him to drive a truck was a Yakima Indian; the man in the next bed in the bunkhouse was a Mexican, a gentle, laughing man, who plunked a battered guitar and sang soft love songs in Spanish.

It wasn't until they had become close friends that he learned that his pal had done a stretch for murder.

He learned, too, the great gulf that exists between the literate and the illiterate, the educated and the uneducated. The college boys looked as tough, and worked as hard, as did the professional migrants.

But a summer job is one thing, and a lifetime of drifting is another. And for the first time since I sent him off to kindergarten, protesting loudly, long years ago, he seemed eager to get back to school.

And, if he only learned that one thing—that books, and the knowledge in them, are not a bore and a burden, but the keys that unlock the doorway to rich, full life in which the mind and not the muscles dominate—then I'll be satisfied.

Galahad Spoke Too Soon

It was the night before Christmas, and all through the house, everybody was stirring, including my cat Galahad. He was limping about from room to room uttering wild soul-wrenching cries, a note of plaintive anguish in his voice. Every once in a while he would go over to the door and squall to be let out. But when somebody went to open the door he would not go out.

He would stand there in the doorway peering out into the dark seeing Lord knows what fierce implacable enemies waiting out there to do him harm.

"He's scared," Mama said. "Every time he goes out, he gets in a fight and gets all scratched up. They bite him and the bites get infected. He won't let me put iodine on his wounds. I tried it once and he almost tore the house down until the iodine quit burning."

"He is a big strong cat," I said. "He ought to fight better. He ought to scratch and bite other cats and make them squall."

"He does fight good," Mama said. "But those cats gang up on him. They don't fight fair."

"Then," I said, "he ought to stay in the house. He ought not to go out at night. . . ."

She looked at me. "Galahad," she said, "cannot help going out at night. He gets lonesome staying in the house. He has to go see his friends. When you hear him wandering around over the house, squalling like that, you know he is lonesome for his friends."

"Girl friends?" I said.

"Who else?" she said.

"Hmmmm," I said. In that case the problem seemed very simple. All we had to do was fix Galahad so he would not get lonesome. At least fix it so he would not know he was lonesome. Then he wouldn't go out and get all chewed up. I slipped out to the telephone.

"Sure," the veterinarian said. "Anytime after the holidays."

"Well," I said, "that's that."

"What's what?" she said.

"Your New Year's present," I said. "I am going to give you a contented cat for a New Year's present."

She thought about this a minute.

"No you don't," she said. "You leave my cat alone."

Over in the corner old Galahad, who had been glaring at me with fierce yellow eyes, gave a triumphant squall. But he spoke too soon.

He got back from the hospital the other day, and I am obliged to report that he is a changed cat. He has taken on a new personality. One of the kids brought him in carrying him in his arms and put him down. The first thing I noticed was the expression on his face.

It had a kind of resigned expression on it. The old devil-may-care glint was gone from his eye. His whiskers seemed to droop. His voice had changed, too. In the old days when Galahad came swaggering in from outdoors where he had been roaming and fighting with great gusto, the first thing he did was utter a great baritone meow, a challenge to all in the house that he was home and tired and sleepy and nobody had better cause him any trouble or he would claw their ear off.

Every time Galahad uttered this war cry, the dog, who was sleeping in front of the register where the hot air comes in, would get up and creep behind the sofa. He did not roam around the house much until old Galahad had been fed and was settled down for a snooze. He did not want to start any trouble.

This time old Galahad did not utter his war cry. He just stood there in the middle of the floor looking at me reproachfully with a sort of hurt look as if to say, "You no-good so-and-so, I think you are responsible for this." Then he gave a sort of plaintive meow like a kitten. This strange sound woke the dog up and he rushed in to see the stranger, figuring probably that it was some small forlorn cat and he would eat him up.

He came roaring into the kitchen and when he saw it was old Galahad that had made this faint noise his astonishment knew no bounds. He walked all around old Galahad investigating him and then went back to his resting place in front of the heat duct. Somehow he seemed to know that his days of crawling behind the sofa until Galahad was pleased to let him come out were over.

Even old Galahad's walk had changed. He does not go about with what Eva calls "that old briskly tail of his" stuck straight up in the air like a spear. He carries it at half-mast. He does not swagger any more and sink his claws into people when they try to fondle him.

He just sleeps. Last night he slept all night. I kept waiting for him to come over and bat me on the nose as was his custom to let me know he was ready to swagger out for a night of roistering. About three o'clock he went to the door and meowed politely and I let him out. He didn't stay five minutes. First thing I knew he was back ready to snooze again. Along about daylight out in the yard I heard a cat squall, a wild, pagan, lonely cry.

"Uh oh," I thought. "That will rouse him."

He didn't even stir.

Graduation Was a Time for Pride

"You will please hold your applause," the principal said, until all the diplomas have been awarded." "Hold my applause!" I whispered to his mother. "I'll hold my breath till he gets his." "Sshshhh," his mother hissed. But he made it all right. They called his name and I sat back and breathed a sigh of relief.

For me the rest was anticlimax. The show was over. He'd made it. He'd mastered those mathematical formulae that for years had bewildered both him and me. He'd parsed those sentences that I, who have to make my living writing, couldn't parse. He'd cut up that baby pig and learned that smattering of French and history and biology.

He'd traveled one road and groping and stumbling he'd found his way triumphantly to its end. Now another rockier road was opening up, the rough and challenging road that leads to a college degree. But I wasn't worried about that. The high school years are the tough years. It is then that the mind drifts in the clouds and learning is a chore and nothing between the covers of a book can be half so fascinating as the world outside the classroom windows.

They didn't call his name when the honors were passed

HAROLD MARTIN REMEMBERS

out. All he got was that little piece of paper and the ring he wore. But I knew how stubbornly he had fought for that much in those long evenings when he bent over his books, while music was beating in his head, and the laughter of good companions and the soft deep roar of a hot rod's exhaust and all those many voices that speak to a man when he is young and strong and the juices of life are surging in him.

And he may be a "rock," as his generation calls a man whose brain does not click like an IBM. But he made it and I was proud of him.

Things Said at Times When You Don't Know What to Say

I heard Mama get up just at daylight, when the birds were beginning to sing, and I lay there listening, and pretty soon I heard him come clumping down the stairs from his room, and I could smell the good smell of coffee in the house. It was the morning he was leaving to go in the army, and I had sort of hoped to get a chance to talk to him and tell him not to worry about anything, but just to take it as it came, day by day, and pretty soon the three years would be over, and he could go back to school for one more term, and get his diploma.

But I'd already gone to bed when he came in, and now the time was growing short and there wouldn't be much time to talk.

So I got up and went out to the kitchen and got a cup of coffee, and sat down with him as he finished his breakfast.

It's a funny thing about fathers: When they don't know what to say to their sons they always ask them how much they weigh.

"How much you weigh?" I asked.

"Two oh eight," he said.

"I weighed 215 when I went in the corps," I said. "They pulled me down to 185 and. . . ."

"Yeah," he said, "you told me about that before."

He picked up the paper and began reading about the stockcar races.

I kept trying to think of something to say. When fathers don't know what to say to their sons, they ask them if they need any money.

"You need any money?" I said.

He shook his head, and kept on reading. "Nope," he said, "I've got ten bucks, that's all I'll need. There won't be a chance to spend anything for about eight weeks. By then maybe I'll have a payday."

"You all packed?" I said. "Where's your suitcase?"

He picked up a little airplane bag beside the chair. "Here's all I need."

He looked at his watch, and sat up.

"Well. So long," he said. He put out his hand. "Take it easy," he said. I took his hand and shook it. I think he thought I might try to kiss him goodbye. He turned quickly toward his mother. "Bye, Ma," he said, and hugged her tight.

I could see her gulp, and her eyes were misty, but she didn't cry. He turned and went out the door, carrying the little bag with his clean shirt, and his socks, and his shaving kit.

"Johnny," she said, "listen to me." He stopped.

"You mind the sergeant," she said.

"Yessum," he said.

Then he was gone.

Pet Raccoon Trees Mr. Cox

Mr. Calvin Cox, one-time city editor of this newspaper, now chief editorial writer, has celebrated his new status by taking on the care and feeding of a pet raccoon named John.

The way I found out about this was by inquiring about four deep scratches which appeared the other morning on Mr. Cox's face, beginning just back of his left eye and moving diagonally downward toward his jaw line.

"Calvin," I said, full of solicitude, "you have the look of a man who has had an altercation with a mother bear in defense of her cubs, or maybe an irate lady subscriber who took offense at one of your editorials."

"No," said Mr. Cox, "it was not a bear nor an irate lady reader. It was my pet 'coon, John, and there was no animosity involved. It was merely a sense of self-preservation on John's part, for which I hold him blameless."

It seems that what happened was this. Every night when Mr. Cox gets home from his day's labors writing learned editorials, he goes out to the backyard to play with John. (He cannot play with John in the house, for pet 'coons are very destructive. They pry into everything. They open cupboards and take all the cans and bottles out and throw them on the floor. They take the caps off of things and pour out the contents. Nobody in his right mind would let a 'coon come into his house.)

So Mr. Cox has to play with John outside, which he was doing when he got lacerated. He was trotting about in the backyard with John sitting on top of his head, making Mr. Cox look like Daniel Boone, or the late Estes Kefauver, wearing a coonskin cap. Unhappily, Mr. Cox, jogging about with John on his head, passed under an overhanging limb, and as he ducked his head to one side, he caused John to lose his balance. John naturally clutched frantically to keep from falling, and with claws extended, he clutched Mr. Cox by the face, raking it deeply.

Despite this, Mr. Cox, who got John from a forest ranger who found him trotting along a mountain road where his mother evidently had abandoned him, is very fond of John. He thinks, in fact, that everybody should own a pet 'coon, and if he can find a mate for John he is thinking of going into the 'coon-raising business.

* * * *

But now he is beginning to have some doubts, for John has raked him across the snoot again, and this time Mr. Cox and the 'coon were thirty feet up a magnolia tree.

"This past weekend," said Mr. Cox, "I came to the conclusion that I should give John a little more freedom. So at great trouble and expense I built him a 'coon run. This was a wire pen about twenty feet long and ten feet wide and five feet high—nicely proportioned, if I do say so myself. It was not in the old tradition of the perfect fence, which was supposed to be horse high, bull strong, and hog tight, but I thought surely it would contain one small and not very vigorous raccoon."

He built the pen, and concreted the floor so John couldn't dig under, and covered the top with wire, and erected a structure in the corner with a sign on it saying, "The 'Coon Room," Mr. Cox being sentimentally attached to the name, he once having patronized a night club called The 'Coon Room which had a girl singer who . . . but never mind.

Anyway, Mr. Cox got up early Sunday morning to find out how John had fared in his new quarters. "I fried him an egg," said Mr. Cox, "since he is very fond of fried eggs for breakfast. But when I went out to take him his egg, there was no sign of him anywhere. He had climbed up one of the supports and found a place where I had forgotten to put a staple. He pushed the wire out, and exited."

Mr. Cox then went all over the neighborhood, calling John, and wafting the fried egg about, hoping that John would smell its aroma and come to him. To no avail.

"The egg got cold, and so did I," said Mr. Cox, "I had given up all hope, and was back in my own front yard when some instinct told me to look up in my magnolia tree. And there, curled up sound asleep, about thirty feet above the ground, was John."

Magnolia trees are easy to climb and Mr. Cox, being an agile man, soon shinnied up to where John was sleeping like a baby.

"John, you rascal you," he rebuked John, reaching out to grab him by the back of the neck.

Raccoons, it seems, wake up fighting when they are aroused suddenly from their rest. So John took a swipe at Mr. Cox, and Mr. Cox, defending his proboscis, which had been left cut and bleeding from this first blow, turned loose the limb he was holding, and John and Mr. Cox together came tumbling out of the magnolia tree, clutching and grabbing at each other and passing limbs as they fell.

No bones were broken in either human or raccoon—

though Mr. Cox did land on John's fried egg, which he had left at the foot of the tree.

"He forgave me, though," said Mr. Cox, "for when I put him back in the pen I gave him a bowl of cornbread and milk, which he likes even better than he likes fried eggs."

A Man Wants His Freedom at Twenty-One

The oldest one came in and said he was going to move. I knew he wasn't mad at me or his mama. It was just that the time had come for him to go. He was his own man now. He was past twenty-one years old. He had a job and was making his own way. It was only natural that he should want his own apartment where he could go and come as he pleased.

I knew how he felt. It's nice to have your own room at home, with your own things in it. It's good to be able to go in and close the door and read or write or play music on the record player. It's nice to have somebody look after your laundry for you, and fix your meals for you.

But it still is living at home. And that is not the way a man wants to live when he is twenty-one years old and earning his own money. He wants his own place, where he is his own master. For you are never on your own completely when you are living in somebody else's house. Even if it is your father's house.

So I didn't try to argue with him. I just went up and watched him as he got his things together—his books and records, and the old guitar. He cleared out the closets and took a picture or two down off the walls. Then he took all this stuff downstairs and loaded it into the car, and took it to the place where he will live.

After he was gone, I felt a little lonely, and a little sad, I must confess. For here was another milestone, one of the inevitable changes that come with time, the shifting of the pattern of a family.

But I didn't argue or protest. A man wants his freedom. And I was actually a little proud of him for wanting to leave. It showed that he had passed a milestone too, that he was ready and willing to go on his own.

So all I told him was Good Luck, and if for any reason he ever wanted to come back again, he'd always be welcome.

Weddings Disrupt Lives of Fathers and Small Dogs

The wedding is over and my dog Shim and I are glad. For pretty soon now everything will be back to normal at our house and we will know where we stand.

Weddings are for mamas and for daughters and for their friends, and for the cook back in the kitchen and her friends. They are not for fathers and for small dogs. All fathers and small dogs are supposed to do is keep out of the way and not hinder those who are caught up in the great complicated ritual with which we surround the simple matter of two people standing up together and telling a preacher that they will love and cherish each other all their days.

In normal times, the father of the family and the family dog live a pretty good life. Their comings and goings are taken note of and they are made to feel welcome and wanted around the house. When they leave in the morning somebody is there at the door to wish them Godspeed. When they come in in the evening somebody is there to scratch them behind the ears, or give them a big lipsticky smacker, whichever is appropriate.

They are permitted to come into the living room where

they can climb up on the sofa and go to sleep, or fall into a favorite chair and read, as it pleases them. At feeding time they are called to the table where they are plied with viands, and afterward, if they wish to go out into the backyard and smoke a pipe and look at the roses, or chase a squirrel or bury a bone, that is their privilege.

In the last hectic days before a wedding all this is changed. Papa and the dog alike go unnoticed. The dog scratches mournfully at the door and nobody lets him in. Papa comes in from work and nobody gives him the big hello. They are all bent over the breakfast room table, looking up street numbers in the telephone book and addressing little white cards and enduring the mental anguish of trying to find a way to fit 200 relatives and dearly beloved friends into a little chapel where there are only 100 seats.

The kindest thing a daughter can do is to run away and get married and then call her parents to tell them that she is ecstatically happy. The next kindest is to have a big church wedding—a joyous come-all-ye where there are seats for everybody. The cruelest is to have a little chapel wedding—"just family and closest friends." For how do you measure one friend against another in terms of a chapel seat? My suggestion that where warmth of friendship was equal, breadth of beam should be the controlling factor, met only with an angry glare.

All these things meant nothing to my dog Shim. He had other harassments. It is the duty of all small dogs to bark at delivery men. In time he comes to know them all—the milk man, the laundry man, the garbage man—and his vocal defense becomes perfunctory. He yaps once or twice, then goes back to sleep. But the days before a wedding drive him crazy. There's always a stranger at the door, bearing packages, telegrams, special delivery letters. He must woof fiercely at them all.

He discovers also that he can no longer snooze where it

pleases him, just as Papa finds out he can no longer smoke his pipe in his chair or go about the house in his undershirt. Mamas get very sensitive to dog hairs and burnt matches and people's undershirts in the days before a wedding. For somebody is always dropping in to see the presents and the house, and Papa must look nice.

Finally, the day arrives that Mama has been looking forward to ever since she heard a mewing birth-cry and the doctor saying, "It's a girl." And all the tension goes out of her, and down the aisle she floats, poised and beautiful and serene. And then here comes Papa in his one brief moment of glory, with a radiant stranger on his arm, unable to believe that this is the same creature he saw that morning, in shorts and halter and scuffed old moccasins, practicing the difficult art of scrambling an egg.

He takes her down to where the groom and best man wait, and finally the preacher says: "Who giveth this woman to be married to this man?" And he isn't supposed to say anything. All he does is take her hand and place it in the preacher's hand.

Then he steps back, being careful not to step on her train, for he has been sternly warned about this. And he slips into the pew by her mother and she pats his hand, and soon he is back home again with nobody fussing at him about his pipe, and the dog is asleep on the sofa and the doorbell is silent. And all is just as it was before except for the empty room upstairs, where she lived for what seems now to have been such a little while.

Sourpuss Better Mind His Manners

It looks as if I am back in the cat business again. I came home from a trip to be greeted at the door by my daughter, holding in her arms a tomcat the size of a small tiger. He also looks like a tiger and I fear he also has the disposition of a jungle cat.

He has a flat broad face, gray, mostly, with fine brown stripes running from his whiskers back over his ears, and he glares at me malevolently from my daughter's arms as if wondering who this stranger is who has come to disrupt the tranquillity of his peaceful days.

"Where," I ask, "did that monster come from?"

"He is not a monster," she says indignantly. "He's sweet. Kiss him."

"I will not kiss him," I say. "I do not kiss cats."

"Well, pet him then," she said, "so he will know you are his friend. Scratch him back of his ears."

And she thrusts this leopard at me so I can scratch him back of his ears, and he reaches out a paw with fishhooks on it and scratches me back of my ear, at the same time going "phhhhttt" and spitting in my eye.

He is, I find out, a wild cat which has been living down in

the woods back of the house, living off the land, so to speak. He has been in a sense a kind of a ghost cat, appearing at the edge of the woods in the evening, looking sorrowfully across the yard as if hungry for human companionship.

And the females of my household are much touched by this. So they get some old shrimp out of the freezer which are getting a little old and mellow and put this shrimp out back of the garden in a little plate. Naturally, after the sun has shone on the shrimp a little while, it begins to attract the cat's attention. So in broad daylight in the middle of the afternoon, he comes out of the woods and gets this shrimp.

He sits very still when my daughter walks up twiddling her fingers at him and saying, "Kitty, kitty, kitty," in a soothing voice. And he makes no protest when she picks him up and brings him into the house. He stalks all over it, inspecting it; and evidently it suits him, for he settles down as if he owns the place.

The dog comes in and starts for him, and he rakes the dog across the nose and puts him in his place. And I come in and he rakes me back of the ear and puts me in my place. And he accepts the cuddling and the loving the female members of my house lavish on him with a bored, disdainful manner, as if this is no more than his due.

But I have got news for this cat. One more "phhhtt" out of him in my direction and he will find himself back down in the woods chasing chipmunks for a living. If he is going to join that long line of notable and distinguished felines—Captain Midnight, Chester, Jr., and Galahad—who have shared my bed and board, he's got to mend his ways. Even then it'll be a long time before I consent to change the name I gave him when I first saw him and which so far fits him well. I call him Sourpuss.

Sourpuss Soared Into a Rosebush

Nothing has changed between me and my new cat, Sourpuss. I stagger in at three o'clock in the morning, after two weeks of wandering around Cuba in pursuit of Mr. Fidel Castro, to find my cat Sourpuss sitting on the front steps glaring at me malevolently. I tell him to move to one side but he makes no move to do so.

So, not wishing to spend the night in the evening dews and damps, I walk straight at him, hoping to intimidate him. He does not intimidate. He goes "pfft" as I approach and hangs a claw in the calf of my leg. I kick at him and miss and very nearly fall down, for it is difficult to kick at a cat while carrying a suitcase in each hand.

He flies around the side of the house, and I go in and am soon sleeping soundly, having had not much sleep in two days of travel. About five o'clock I hear a crash out in the living room and a frantic twittering. I rush out barefooted and peer around dazedly in the cold, gray dawn, thinking perhaps a burglar is in the house.

At first I do not see anything. Then a frantic peeping and fluttering comes from the corner. The parakeet's cage, which was on a table, has been knocked to the floor.

Sourpuss is up on top of the cage reaching through with his paw and swiping fiercely at the parakeet, which is cowering in terror just out of reach of the fishhooks that are flashing past his nose.

I seize him by the scruff of the neck, avoiding his claws, and carrying him at arm's length I take him to the back door and fling him into the yard. He lands on his feet unhurt, of course, and stands there with his back up glaring at me balefully. A squirrel in the oak above his head jerks his tail and cusses him. I put the parakeet cage back on the table, cover it with its cover and go back to bed.

Fifteen minutes later there is the same sound re-enacted—a crash and a terrified twittering. Again I rush out. There on the floor is the cage, and on top of it is the cat swiping fiercely at the parakeet. I begin to think I am caught in some weird repetitious nightmare. Again I pick up the cat, and this time I put all I've got into the heave. He sails through the air about thirty feet and comes down in the middle of a rosebush. It was not my intention to throw him into the rosebush, but a man throwing a tomcat does not have time to take aim. The idea is to throw the cat before he can sink his claws in.

I noticed he turned in midair and landed on his feet in the rosebush.

Then I locked the basement door, where he had been sneaking in to assault the parakeet, and went back to bed. He went off somewhere, I suppose, to pick the rose thorns out of his epidermis.

I know, of course, that many nice old ladies will write me, telling me I am a brute. But I know who is the brute around my house. It is that cat.

He Needed Help to Pass the Cat

There was one bright ray of sunshine blazing through the dining room window, striking the floor of the hall just in front of the open door leading into the living room. Lying in this shaft of sunshine was my tomcat, Sourpuss, solemn as the Sphinx. He wasn't sleeping. He was just crouched there in the warm yellow light, his paws curved in a little circle against his chest, his cold yellow eyes half closed.

People came and went through the door and they sidled around him, or stepped over him, murmuring an apology. He did not blink an eye or move a whisker.

I heard my dog Shim scratch at the back door. I opened the door and he came in at a limping trot, still lame from an old fight. He nodded and snuffled and wagged a polite "thank you" to me as he passed by, for he is a mannerly dog. But he didn't stop to have his ears scratched. It was cold and windy outside and he was headed for the living room and his warm spot on the sofa.

Then he saw the cat lying there blocking the way he would have to pass before he could get his rest. He stopped. He stood a long time, looking at the cat. He did not look like a dog who has just come upon a cat unexpectedly and is suddenly filled with a desire to assault this cat. He looked like a dog who would be perfectly well satisfied not to see another cat as long as he lived on earth.

I could read what was running through his mind. "There is that blank blank cat," he was thinking. "I have got to get past him. If I try to jump over him he may damage me beyond repair. If I try to sneak past him, he'll sink a claw into me as I go by."

With a funny sidling gait that looked as if he was trying to tiptoe he moved toward the cat, but his eyes rolled sideways, watching. The cat didn't turn his head. But the green eyes narrowed a little and at the very tip the cat's tail twitched, once, twice. Shim saw that twitch and he'd been around cats long enough to know it meant danger. He stopped and looked back over his shoulder at me imploringly.

"Okay," I said. "Okay. Come on, and I'll lead you by."

I went over and stood in front of the cat, very close. The cat lay motionless, staring at my ankles. Slowly, as if he were moving past a coiled rattlesnake, Shim crept by, keeping me between him and the cat. His back end was tucked up as if any minute he expected to feel the hot needles of the cat's claws stab him. He started to run as he got past, hit the sofa with a thump, turned around three times and lay down with a sigh. He had the foolishest grin on his face you ever saw. The cat still looked like the Sphinx. One more cold war crisis was past.

The Old and the Gray

I don't know who is the more frustrated, me or that squirrel. The war between us has been going on for over a week now—with his winning a few skirmishes and my winning a few, and unless one of us gives in, it may go on until we both are old and gray. As a matter of fact, I already am. He's just gray.

The whole thing started when Mama decided that the bird feeder had hung by the back door long enough. Everybody that comes to the house comes in the back door, and by now they were wading ankle deep through the empty shells of sunflower seeds and feathers. And other items. Birds are very untidy eaters. Chipmunks were always scurrying about, too, eating the seeds the birds had dropped onto the ground, and some of our friends, ladies of nervous disposition, did not look forward to approaching the entry, knowing they would flush a covey of chipmunks.

The good thing about the feeder's being in this place, though, was that anybody working at the kitchen sink could see the birds close up. It was one of those long glass tubes with six perches on it, and there was always a swirl of birds around it. A chickadee wearing his little black cap down over his ears would be replaced by a titmouse with his topknot. Sometimes a cardinal would swoop in wearing a black mask like a burglar. And now and then a huge flicker, with the red smear on his cheeks making him look as if he had cut himself shaving. He had to feed at the bottom holes so that his long tail, which he uses to brace with, could curl up under the tube. Goldfinches came, and grosbeaks, and fourteen million sparrows of every species, all of them alike, and all a little different. So there was always a show at the kitchen window in the whirl and flash of many wings.

The squirrels could get to the feeder too, but it didn't matter, for they were easy to scare off. Miss Eva would be standing at the sink washing dishes, and as soon as a squirrel came along the window sill and climbed onto the feeder, she would holler at him: "Shoo! Shooh! Scoot!" she would yell, and rap on the window and the squirrel would leap off in alarm and go scurrying across the yard, his tail jerking angrily. Sometimes when Miss Eva thought of it, she would take the nozzle she sprays dishes with and squirt hot water on the squirrel. A squirrel looks very surprised and jumps for a great distance when you squirt hot water on his backside. Or cold water either, for that matter.

But it was a messy place, so I moved the feeder around to the backyard and hung it between two trees, right outside a window, so I could sit and look out at the feeding birds. I hung it on a wire, and for two days I didn't see a bird on it. They would fly around it all right, but they were afraid to land, for always there was this big fat slob of a squirrel, hanging upside down on it, stuffing himself. He'd trot out along that wire as nonchalantly as if he were walking on solid ground.

Then somebody told me that if I used a flat tape instead of a wire, he couldn't walk across on that. It would turn under his feet, and he'd fall off. So I strung the feeder on a tape, the thin, flat, rubber and wire tape people use to connect TV sets with the antenna.

The first visitor was a cardinal. He lit on the tape and sat there while he inspected the feeder. Or rather he tried to sit on it. But the tape turned and twisted under his feet so that he had to jerk his tail and flutter his wings furiously, trying to keep his balance. Then he flew off.

"Boy, oh boy," I said to myself. "This is the answer. If this thing is so twisty even a bird can't sit on it, my old bushy-tailed friend is out of business."

When I think about how wrong I was I feel like bursting into sobs.

I was sitting there by the window, waiting to gloat, when the first squirrel came down the tree from which the feeder hung. He saw the tape nailed to the tree, stood there looking at it and looking at the feeder beyond. His tail jerked rhythmically, and I could tell he was deep in thought. He started out on the tape, gingerly, and it began to wobble under him, and he turned back to the tree. The vigor with which his tail began to jerk indicated that he was losing his temper. Evidently he figured that the bold attack would be the best. He put his front paws on the tape, like a tightwire walker testing his footing, adjusted himself to the rhythm of the wobble, and dashed out. All at once there was a blur of gray—grabbing, clutching, over and under and over and under again, his tail whipping desperately from side to side, he struggled to hang on. And he hung. He ended up upside down, but he discovered that from this position the tape could not flip out from under him, so he proceeded nonchalantly on to the feeder and clung there, head down, holding himself by his hind feet and his tail, as with his forepaws and his narrow underjaw he rifled the feeder of its seed.

So I went then and got a couple of pie plates and strung them on the tape, on each side of the feeder. And these seemed to worry him, for he climbed the tree and hung there, upside down, jerking his tail and chattering angrily. And then he launched himself backward through the air, and turned in flight, and came down so close to the feeder he tipped it with a paw and set it swinging. I went out and measured the distance, and he had jumped, from a standing start, a distance of seventy-eight inches. So I moved the feeder a foot or so in the other direction. But this put it just a few feet away from a strawberry pot on the edge of the terrace and before I could get back into the house he had launched himself from the strawberry pot and was back on the feeder, stuffing himself. I went out and moved the strawberry pot, which weighed just a little less than a ton. And when my wife saw what I had done, she made me move it back. Which meant I had to move the feeder again.

But before I did, I watched old Piggy, the squirrel, for awhile. He had decided he'd try it from the ground this time. He sat there under the feeder, looking up, and he was like an athlete, working himself up to a great effort. He held his paws in front of his face, rubbing them together as if he had spat on them and then he launched himself straight up. He went up with one paw outstretched, like an outfielder leaping for a fly ball that is going over the fence. And again, he just tipped the bottom of the feeder. I went out and measured again. He'd jumped forty-five inches straight up.

Then he tried traveling along the tape again, going through the same mad gyrations as before. And this time he discovered that by hanging upside down he could push the pie plates ahead of him with his nose until he got to the feeder.

So I resolved to shoot the works. I went to the hardware store and got swivels to attach to the trees, so that the tape would start whirling as soon as he stepped on it. I got fishing leaders, thirty-pound test, and attached them to the tape and to the handle of the feeder. I strung pie plates all along the route, stapled together so he could not push them with his nose, or crumple them, or climb over, around, or under them.

And for awhile this stopped him. He'd go out and do his wild balancing act and then go back to the tree, cussing and jerking his tail. So I decided to try one last dirty trick on him. I went to the store and invested $1.79 in a foul-smelling powder, a mixture of napthalese and nicotine, which is supposed to repel dogs and rabbits and keep them away from plants. I figured if it would do this, it would also repel squirrels. So I made up a paste of this stuff and smeared it around the place where the tape was attached to the tree. And whether it repelled him or stimulated him, I don't know. All I know is, he walked right through it and stood there on the tree looking at the feeder for a second. And then again, he launched himself backward, turning in midair, coming down this time, kerwhoomp, right on top of the feeder. And the fishing leader snapped, and he and the feeder went down together with a thump and a clatter of tin pie plates. He got up and ran off a few steps, and then stopped and thought a moment. Then he came back to the fallen feeder and began to stuff himself.

I was sitting there, with my head in my hands, when Miss Eva came in. She saw the squirrel. She went over and banged on the window and yelled "Shoo, Scoot." And he scooted. "That old squirrel," said Miss Eva, "know not to mess with me."

Now I know the only solution to my problem. I'll put an effigy of Miss Eva in the window, rigged up with some sort of electric eye that will set off a recording of Miss Eva hollering "Shoo," every time a squirrel comes in sight.

Small Speckled Bird Found Dazed on Sidewalk

It wasn't the great speckled bird of song and legend; it was a small speckled bird—a brown thrasher, it looked like to me—and what it was doing sitting on the sidewalk beside the Atlantan Hotel, I do not have the foggiest notion.

When we first saw it, an Ivy-looking character in a narrow brimmed hat and a sincere suit, carrying a tightly furled umbrella, was stooping over peering at it. And I thought perhaps he was going to pick it up and take it somewhere, safely out of the way of the passing foot traffic. But I was watching him in the rear view mirror, and he didn't, so I asked Mama, who was driving me to the airport, to circle the block. She did, and we came back, and the little bird was still sitting there, with the passersby looking but hardly breaking stride as they passed him.

He was sitting there with his eyes closed, standing up straight, not crouched, and when I reached down and he felt my fingers closing around him he came suddenly to life. His wings beat hard, and his eyes opened, and he made a harsh scratching cry. But as I held him as gently as I could, he settled down all of a sudden and shut his eyes again. So I put him on the floor in the back of the car and he sat there quietly.

He was still sitting there, placidly enough, sick, or stunned, or whatever, when I got out at the airport.

The next day when I got back home, I got a full report. The bird, Mama said, had slept in the back of the car all the way home, and when she got there, she tried to look him up in the bird book. He was a soft brown on his head and back, and his chest was white, streaked with dark brown, like a brown thrasher. But instead of having a long tail like a thrasher, he had a short, broad tail like a thrush. Thrush or thrasher or whatever, his habitat certainly was not the sidewalks of downtown Atlanta. Both are dwellers in bosky dells, in leafy glades, in quiet places under bushes where bugs creep in the leaf mold.

Mama got a spoon and gave him some water, which he seemed to enjoy. Then she offered him some egg yolk, which he ignored. So she took him out and put him under the sasanqua bush, where a great many brown thrashers are usually to be seen hopping about in search of nourishment.

He flew strongly as she turned him loose, then came back and landed on a limb in the holly bush. And there she left him, peering about a little dazedly, his eyes falling shut and then opening again.

She watched him a while, and he didn't do anything. Then she left to get the groceries, and when she came back he was gone. Good luck to him.

Old Shim Knew His Time Had Come

Old Shim made his last journey to the hospital the other day, a few days before what would have been his eighteenth birthday. Usually he went willingly, for he had been there so many times in recent years he was not afraid.

Mama would help him out of the back seat of the car, and he would head straight for the hospital door; she'd open it for him and he'd go in and stand there for a moment looking around.

His old eyes, turned milky with cataracts, could not see much, but his nose told him who was there: a big yellow cat glaring balefuly from his owner's arms, a little black poodle with a topknot, peering with black shoe-button eyes at him, standing shortlegged, broad-backed and shaggy in the door.

Then, ignoring them all, he would walk slowly, like a tired old man, his toe-nails scritch-scratching on the linoleum floor, to the glassed-in office where the young lady at the admissions desk would speak to him amiably and check him in.

She didn't have to ask any questions. She had known him a long time, and he knew her, and he stood still as she leaned down to pat him.

Then he would turn and go down the hall, stopping at the open door of each room to peer in, looking for his friend, Will, the old man who had fed and watered and bathed him and seen to his comfort when he had come to the hospital before.

Then, when he had seen Will and had been spoken to, he would continue his investigation, looking for his other friend, the doctor.

He wasn't afraid at all, for he knew that here there were friendly hands and gentle voices. The little needles might stick him, but the pain was soon over, and always, they made him feel better.

When he came home, his coat was glossy, his aches and pains were gone, and for a few days he was almost frisky again.

But the years are not to be denied, and an old dog who is stone deaf, and toothless, and nearly blind, who suffers with asthma, and arthritis, and the loss of memory that affects old dogs as well as old people, does not get better for long.

He began to sleep more and more, and he found it harder and harder to get up from his bed and go out.

Sometimes, lately, when it was gray and misty outside, or a little cold, he'd stand in the back door for a moment, sniffing, and then he would turn back to his bed even though it was early morning, and he already had had a long night's sleep.

Just before he made his last journey, though, he got so he couldn't sleep. His dreams seemed to trouble him, and he would cry in his sleep, and then he would get up and walk all over the house, bumping into things and whimpering.

Mama would get up and sit up with him, petting him and soothing him until he was ready to go back to sleep again. Sometimes she was up nearly all night with him.

So finally, she took him, in love and pity, to the hospital. This time, he seemed to know that there was something different about the journey. He did his best to make it seem he was all right again.

He didn't lie down on the seat of the car and sleep on the way to the hospital the way he usually did. He sat up and put his nose out the window and let the wind blow in his face, as he used to do when he was a young dog.

And when she took him out of the car and put him down, he almost trotted to the hospital door. But when he got inside, he suddenly stopped, and turned, and went back out the open door, and gathering all his strength, he tried to jump back into the car again.

And when she took him in her arms into the waiting room, he did not ignore the cats and the dogs who were waiting there; his neck hairs rose, and he growled deep, and when she put him down, instead of going to find his friend, the doctor, he turned and tried to get back to the car again.

But the gentle hands came and took him, as they had so many times before, and did everything they could for him.

Then, after a day or two, the doctor called and said that there wasn't much else that he could do to make him easy and comfortable again. Except one thing.

So we made the decision, and later, without any pain at all, and with no fear, old Shim went to sleep.

The Queen's First Birthday

I stayed home the other day to observe the second generation at my house, namely, Miss Mary Hamilton Bell, otherwise known as the Queen of Love and Beauty, celebrate her first birthday with a cake and a candle and a gathering of her friends.

They weren't her friends exactly, for when you are one year old you haven't had time to make many friends. But they were children of her mama's friends, and they were all about the same age, so everything went off all right.

There was some squalling, but there weren't any real fights, though some people did get pushed down. It doesn't matter much if you get pushed down when you are one year old, for your bottom is very close to the ground when you are that age, and you are very well padded anyhow.

The Queen received her guests standing out in the backyard, and she greeted them by reaching out and feeling of them, and sometimes by trying to rub her nose against theirs. They responded by getting behind their mamas' skirts, or their nurses' skirts, and peering around at the Queen very solemnly.

Then, when she was not paying any attention, they came

out of hiding and poked at her, and attempted to feel of her, for this seems to be the way that babies get acquainted when they are that age.

I had not paid much attention to one-year-old babies up to now, but I studied these at some length and I have come to the conclusion that some lampshade manufacturer is now making little girls' clothes. All the dresses were shaped like lampshades.

They flare out wide under the arms and then chop off short just about the knees, which makes all little girl babies look like characters out of that cartoon strip called B. C.

Little boys, of course, do not wear dresses when they are one year old; they wear little white suits, and all of them have square feet. I think the people who make baby shoes learned their trade making shoe boxes.

Or maybe it is because little boys just naturally have square feet.

I also noticed that very few of the little girls wore ribbons in their hair. I had thought all little girls wore ribbons in their hair, but one of the nurses explained why they didn't.

"No use putting a ribbon in a child's hair when she is going to a party," she said. "First thing some other child does is snatch it out."

I was pleased to see that when time to eat the cake and ice cream came, the Queen of Love and Beauty was the perfect hostess. She demonstrated the proper way to eat ice cream. She got her plate off the table and sat down on the floor with it. She pushed the cake and ice cream off the plate onto the floor with her hand. Then she ate them with her spoon.

All her little guests were well trained enough to know that you follow your hostess' example in such matters. So they plopped down on the floor with their plates, too. Fortunately, it was a linoleum floor and had been freshly scrubbed, so possibly no great harm was done.

The germ theory does not seem to work where small

children are concerned. They spend half their time chewing on something they have found on the floor.

It was a nice, quiet party that left the house littered with colored balls and music boxes and wooden ducks and chickens on rollers, that quack or cackle when you pull them on a string. And a baby sleeping seraphically, worn out by her duties as a hostess.

And I hope I am around next year when it happens again.

Idiot Towhee Feeds Cowbirds As if They Were Her Own

If I weren't afraid the Humane Society would get after me, I would bounce a rock off that mama towhee that has a nest somewhere in the depths of my spirea bush. She is an idiot. She does not know as much about birds as I do, and she is one of them. She can't even tell the difference between a towhee and a cowbird. Or maybe her maternal instinct is so strong she just does not care.

The first time I noticed this curious lack of intelligence in this particular towhee was about a week ago when she landed lightly in the middle of my backyard. Plunking down beside her, fluttering and flogging the air as they landed, were three young birds. One was obviously her own child, a slender long-tailed girl towhee, newly fledged out. The other two were bigger and burlier, shorter of tail and more compactly built, grayish instead of brownish in their juvenile plumage, but with the brown sheen just starting on their heads that marked them as cowbirds, not towhees.

The birds were scattered all over the yard, a new system I worked out to foil the squirrels. I used to fill the bird feeders, and the thrashers would come and thrash around and spill the seed out on the ground, and the squirrels and the chipmunks would come sit under the feeders and eat up all the seeds from the ground-feeding birds. So I started scattering the feed over the yard, putting it in little clusters here and there. This gives all the birds a chance and makes the squirrels work for a living.

So, everybody was having dinner. The mama cardinals were feeding their babies, and the thrashers were feeding theirs, and the blue jays, whose babies evidently haven't left the nest yet, were filling their beaks with seeds and flying off home to feed their young. Each to his own. Except that silly towhee. The two cowbird babies shoved her own baby out of the way and stuck their open beaks up to be fed, and she fed them, while the little towhee had to forage for himself.

There was only one bright spot in the whole thing. One of the young cowbirds wandered over to where a mama thrasher was feeding her young and opened his beak to be fed, and the mama thrasher took one look at him and pecked him on top of the head so hard it knocked him bowlegged. That seemed to teach him something, for he staggered off and started feeding himself. Now if the mama towhee will give his brother the same treatment. . . .

The King Is Gone; Long Live the King

Ever since I mentioned in this space that my cat, Old Sourpuss, had walked out one morning and had never come back, nice people have been calling up to tell me that they were sorry about Old Sourpuss, and offering me a cat as a replacement. I thought this was a nice neighborly gesture on their part and I appreciated it, but the feeling around the house was that maybe we would just be without a cat for a while.

Down the years there has been a parade of cats—Captain Midnight, Chester, Jr., Sir Galahad, and, finally, Old Sourpuss, the roughest, toughest, ugliest, surliest of them all, but with a heart of gold.

With the departure of Sourpuss, we figured maybe it was time to take a vacation from cats for a while.

But you know how these things are. And right now, back in the laundry room, there is the runtiest, sickliest, scrawniest little old yellow kitten you ever saw, sleeping soundly with his tummy full of milk. How he got there, as I piece the story together, was this:

The other day a neighbor of mine from down the street who loves birds and hates cats because she claims they catch birds, which is not so, called up to say that there was a cat under her hydrangea bush and would somebody who knew about cats come see about it.

So Mama and Miss Nancy went down there, slopping through the wet, for it was raining, both of them saying, "Now whatever happens, we will not get involved with this cat, for we do not need any more cats for a while."

Then they see it. The lady who does not like cats actually has a heart as big as a watermelon, so she has put the cat in a box in the greenhouse, where it would keep warm. And there it lay, wet and muddy and mewing faintly and so weak from hunger it couldn't hold up its head.

So the next thing they know, Mama and Nancy are back home with this cat. They wash it gently and dry it good and it turns out to be a beautiful cat with yellow fur and deep burnt orange stripes. And they hold some milk up close to its nose and it laps it feebly, and pretty soon it is full of milk, but still so puny it cannot stand up.

But that was day before yesterday. Yesterday, still tottering a little but going fast, it began to walk around. And today I was sitting there reading when I heard a loud meow, and I looked up and there was this cat, striding across the living room as if he owns the place.

Then he sat down in the middle of the rug, and began to wash his face, and then he yawned and looked about, hunting for a quiet place to curl up and go to sleep.

So it looks as if Old Sourpuss, may he rest in peace even though nobody else ever could while he was around, has got a successor.

Fat Tassie Forgives

My friend Fat Tassie Fitzsimmons, the corpulent and elderly blue-tick hound which lives across the street, is a little put out with me. Tassie spends a great deal of time at my house, lying spread-eagled on the welcome mat at the back door. The welcome mat is made out of a stiff plastic that imitates grass, and when Tassie wiggles about on it, it scratches her underside, which pleases Tassie very much, for if there is anything she dearly loves it is getting scratched. She comes over in the afternoon, when I am sitting out in the backyard, talking to somebody, or reading a book, and half apologetically, but very insistent, she comes up and nuzzles my hand, rubbing her head against it, begging to be scratched.

So, I pull her ears and scratch behind them, and then scratch down her back and along her flanks, and she stands there with this blissful look on her face, and I think if I kept on scratching she'd stand there forever. Sometimes, though, she gets so carried away that she will light out running in a big circle around the chairs, not barking, but wearing this look of idiot delight, and when other people are there, they look at her as if she were out of her mind.

HAROLD MARTIN REMEMBERS

Tassie, of course, is not unaware of her debt to people who scratch her and make her happy, and she repays them by seeing that they are protected from wild creatures that might do them harm, such as chipmunks, sparrows, jaybirds, squirrels, and wayfaring dogs from down the street. Tassie will lie for hours on the welcome mat or in the liriope border, liriope being a heavy stiff grass that she finds is also very good for scratching her undercarriage. Chipmunks go scurrying past her nose on whatever important mission chipmunks always seem to be on, and birds of a dozen different feathers peck all around her at the seed we have scattered in the grass, and squirrels are all over the place, and wandering dogs come by and greet Tassie amiably, and she greets them. And none of these things worry her at all.

The moment we pull in the driveway, though, all this changes. Tassie leaps up from where she has been snoozing and goes bounding across the yard barking furiously, putting birds to flight, and sending squirrels up trees in great haste, and sending the chipmunks skittering, tails straight up, to their snug burrows beneath the bricks of the terrace. And if a neighborhood dog comes ambling up to pass the time of day while she is on her fearless watchdog mission, she turns on him with a snarl and a growl and chases him out of the yard. Then, looking very proud of herself, she comes back as if to say to us "Okay. You're safe now."

That's the way it was until a few days ago, when this misunderstanding rose between me and Tassie. It was early in the morning, and I came out the back door in a hurry; and not knowing that Tassie was asleep on the welcome mat, I stepped smack on her. Suddenly something hard and soft and rough and smooth all at the same time was rolling under my foot and I didn't know what it was until Tassie let out a yelp and nipped me on the ankle. And I, in my surprise, let out a yell and kicked Tassie, and said harsh words to her. And she went home, looking back over her shoulder mournfully, and hasn't been back since to be scratched behind the ears. She's a good old dog, though, and evidently does not hold a grudge, for I just talked to Mama on the phone and she said when she drove in Tassie was there running all over the yard again protecting her from the chipmunks and sparrows.

So I guess I am forgiven.

Queen's New Trick Guaranteed To Make Anybody Feel Silly

I don't know where she learned this little trick. Maybe peeping at people when they didn't know she was there. Anyway, the other night I was looking in the bookcase for a book when the Queen came over and grabbed me by the thumb and pulled and said, "COME HERE!" (She talks in capital letters and spaces her words as if she is thinking about them before she speaks.)

"Come here,—*please*," I say.

I think all little babies should learn to say please. This gets you in trouble sometimes though, for babies are always asking for something, and you tell them that they can't have it unless they say please. So they say "please" and you give it to them, if it is something they are supposed to have. But if it's something they can't have, such as a razor blade or something, and they say "please" and you still won't let them have it, this confuses them and makes them angry.

Anyway, as I started to say before I got sidetracked, she grabbed me by the thumb and led me over to a big easy chair and said, "SIT DOWN." So I sat down and she went trot trot trot off to the kitchen and came back leading her grandmother by the thumb. She led her over to the chair where I was sitting and said, as if she would brook no nonsense, "SIT DOWN." So her grandmother sat down in my lap, which was the only place to sit, and once this was accomplished the Queen issued another order.

"MAKE LOVE!" she commanded. So I gave her grandmother a smooch on the ear, thinking this will suffice, and her grandmother gave me a small smooch on the ear. But this did not seem to be what the Queen had in mind. She scrambled up in both our laps and grabbed her grandmother's ear with one hand and my ear with another and pushed our noses together.

"MAKE LOVE!" she ordered. Then, as if we were dull people who have to be instructed in such matters, she announces "WE MAKE LOVE!" So everybody has to give everybody else a smacker, and it is a very silly business, and I am happy nobody else was there to see it.

But the Queen seemed to enjoy it very much. And she remembered it. For the next morning early, when I had gulped my coffee and grabbed my briefcase, and had given her grandmother a goodbye peck, I was half way out the back door when I heard her yell, "COME HERE," and she led me back in and over to the chair where her grandmother was still sleepily sipping her coffee and reading the paper, with her face not fixed yet, and said, "SIT DOWN."

So I sat down, and again the Queen climbed up in the chair and shouted, "MAKE LOVE!" and started all this smooching.

And at this time of morning it IS a silly business.

The Years Fall Away

I have just spent two days and nights with the happiest woman you ever saw. She burbled, she chortled, she laughed and made funny faces, and did a little dance now and then. And she picked up heavy objects from the floor, and carried them about, singing little songs to them, completely disregarding the fact that her back had been giving her some trouble lately. At the end of two days and nights she was so tired that she was almost ready to collapse. But she was very, very happy.

If you have jumped to the conclusion that somebody near and dear to me has suddenly become bereft of her reason, you would be only half right. She is near and dear to me all right, for we have been married for I can't remember how many years. But the reactions I described are not those of somebody who has lost her marbles. They are the natural reaction of a grandmother when she gets a chance to look after her grandchildren for a couple of days while their parents are busy moving into a new house and cannot have them underfoot for fear the moving men will step on them.

The transformation was amazing. The years fell away. The boredom that afflicts us all as we become sexagenarian was suddenly ended. She was no doting grandmother fussily buying little presents at the store, but a busy and bustling young mother-figure blowing noses, changing diapers, mediating squabbles, anointing bottoms with healing oil, and spanking others when they needed it. And doing it all with the greatest zest and joy.

The somewhat startled recipients of these ministrations were two little girls—twins five years old—and their little brother, named Farrell the Barrel when he came bellowing into the world twelve months ago, and whose name has become even more appropriate since.

There was one thing I noticed about her. She adapted quickly to the new and easier ways by which modern young mothers raise their babies. When Farrell the Barrel's father was also fat and barrel-shaped and one year old, she would get up in the night to see if he had kicked the covers off, which he always had. Now they just put babies to bed in sleeping clothes so warm they don't have to have any covers. She also sat with Farrell's papa when he ate, stuffing food into his kisser with a spoon. Farrell's plate was put down before him, his food chopped up in bits and pieces and he picked it up with his hands and ate. The idea behind this is simple. They don't learn to use their hands if you feed them with a spoon. Let them eat with their hands a while and then hand them a spoon, and they master it in no time.

I noticed, though, that some things did not change. When it came time to change a diaper she whomped him down on his back on the bed and when he began to bawl and thrash about she reached far back into her memory and began to sing the little song she used to sing to the Barrel's father when he was getting his diaper changed (boy, is he going to hate me for this). It was a song that was something about a train and the best I can remember it started "My mommy done tole me, when I was in knee pants, my mommee done tole me, Son. A woman's a two face, worrisome thing that'll leave you to sing the blooooze . . . in the night. . . ." Then she'd go "Ah whoooeee a whoooeee," and when she made this sound like a lonesome whistle blowing, he'd get so excited he couldn't stand it. He would kick and gurgle and sputter and laugh, and she'd finish the pinning and grab him up and hold him close and laugh, too, out of the sheer joy of being a grandmother playing at being a mother again.

Just Sit Back and Enjoy

First, there was the Queen and I thought, man, this is something. Nobody could ask more out of life than to be the grandfather of somebody as beautiful and bright and warm and cute and wise and funny as this one. . . .

And then the twins arrived, and it is very difficult not to conclude that two babies, who look almost exactly alike, are not just twice as cute and funny and lovable and laughable as one baby, but by reacting to each other, they are about four times as funny and laughable and lovable and mischievous as one baby, for they can think of four times as many things to do.

They are visiting on Sunday, for example, and are sitting in their highchairs eating dinner with as much solemnity and dignity as the grownups. Then all of a sudden, with a blue-eyed twinkle and a flash of rice-grain teeth and a laugh, one of them takes up a spoonful of potato souffle and plops it down on top of her head and the other one observes this; and with a great happy laugh, she does the same thing, and while their mama is trying to get the potato souffle out of their hair, scolding them fiercely in loving exasperation, I exercise that happiest of prerogatives that goes with grandparenthood—the right not to get involved in such cheerful fracases. So I sit back and laugh, and they seem very pleased to have made their grandpa laugh.

And now a new moment of high excitement in the grandparent business is approaching. Old Skip, who has not been home in five years or thereabouts, is coming from Finland en route to a new assignment in London, bringing my first grandson, whom I have never seen but whom I have already nicknamed Big John the Second, for from his pictures he is as big and fat and jolly as the uncle for whom he is named was when he was a baby. And I can't wait to get them all together and turn them loose in a sandpile in the backyard. For there is nothing more fascinating than to watch babies watching each other when they meet for the first time. When they are grandbabies that is, and their parents are there to blow noses and whack bottoms and put down fights, and all you have to do is sit back and, as Harry Golden says, enjoy, enjoy.

* * * *

And so we did enjoy, as the years moved on. And more grandchildren came—and more cats. There was the matronly old cat we named Mrs. Gray, a stranger who came out of the woods, walked over our house, inspecting it, and then went back to the wildwood and brought back three little spike-tailed kittens—a pink one with blue eyes, a black and white, and a shy little mouse-gray fellow.

And later a mama cat named "Mrs. Unfriendly" showed up, and had her kittens in the laundry basket, on top of my shirts. She was killed soon after by a fuzzy old dog from down the street, which meant that Mama ended up feeding three kittens with an eyedropper until the Humane Society, may their name be blessed, took over the task.

And the grandbabies kept coming, too. John, who was called Juan by his Spanish mother, was referred to as

"Po-sol" by Miss Eva, who looked upon all babies as "poor souls" until they grew old enough to assert themselves, and later became known to the family as "Don Juan Po-Sol." And he was joined by a tiny brunette beauty who soon earned the nickname of Hurricane Sonja. With Don Juan Po-sol also came a small fluffy dog, born in Warsaw, who understood only Polish. Her name was Is'kra, meaning "Sparky," and to get her to come into the house I had to stand in the back door yelling "Is'kra—Hotch tu" meaning "Come here"—which made me feel foolish.

Our youngest, Miss Twinkle, and her husband Dave Sparks, came home, bringing a cat named Sidney, an apartment-raised calico female which had never seen a creature bigger and more formidable than a cockroach, and who found herself greatly puzzled and alarmed by all the creatures around our house. Sidney turned out to be the only cat I ever knew who would answer the call of a mockingbird. When feeding time came Miss Twinkle would call "Sidneeeee" in a thin high-pitched voice, and the mockingbird heard this and learned to imitate it perfectly. So he would toll Sidney off into the woods, thinking he was to be fed.

Soon another granddaughter arrived, Miss Pamela Sparks, and after her, a little brother, Mike.

And pretty soon they all were gone, cats and grandchildren and house dogs and all. But there were still the squirrels and the chipmunks, the doves, and the blue jays and the cardinals and the mockingbirds—and a half dozen neighborhood dogs, who dropped by every afternoon, just to bow and snuffle, and get scratched behind the ears.

So life went on, warm with friendship, rich with fond memories—of cats and dogs and children and all manner of creatures, great and small.